Michael was brought up in a strict environment by his father, Paddy. He was born in the northern English mill town of Oldham in 1957. Both his father and the Catholic Church had a significant influence on his upbringing, which influenced how he behaved as a teenager.

Contents

Paddy's Power

Author: Michael Connolly

Irishtown

Patrick Connolly, better known as Paddy, was only sixteen years old when he left his hometown of Irishtown in County Mayo in western Ireland. Along with Uncle Thomas, he embarked on a journey that would last a lifetime. All he knew was that they'd be working together in Oldham, a North West England industrial town. Because his father's farm was in decline, the majority of Paddy's hard-earned money was sent back to Ireland to assist with the general upkeep of the property.

.

Great Britain felt dread and apprehension in 1937 as Adolf Hitler, the German chancellor, was getting ready to build up his army to wage war throughout Europe. For the previous two years, his sister had been attending school in Oldham to become a midwife. He moved in with her and worked very hard to fix Manchester's roads up until the anticipated start of the war in 1939. From that point on, he travelled to Lincoln and Hereford to work on farms to support the war effort.

He returned to Oldham five years after the war ended to continue working while also making frequent trips to Ireland to support his father's farm with the money he was earning. Paddy adjusted to life in England as it began to recover from World War II. In 1951, he was having a drink at his favourite pub, The White Swan, after work when he witnessed a woman named Madeline pass out. As fate would have it, it was the beginning of the remainder of Paddy's life. Shortly after bringing her home, he made her an engagement proposal.

He married her in 1953, when they gradually fell in love. They had a son named Patrick a year later, and Paddy celebrated by repeatedly announcing that he "had a son" in the same pub where he initially met his wife. It was a joyous time for him. Christine, Michael, John, and Maureen were the following four children, in that Paddy and Madeline established a tradition in which he would proudly visit his family in Ireland to introduce each child to his parents, siblings, and grandparents.

Because I was the middle child, I visited Ireland three times. I, on the other hand, was only seven years old when Maureen was born, and that was the only occasion I could recall. My parents must have had a difficult journey with four children, luggage, and an infant in tow. It involved taking a train to Holyhead, a ferry to Dublin, and then trains to County Mayo, but as Paddy muttered before we left, "We'd make it because God is travelling with us," followed by the sign of the cross, I believe he was holding us up because I didn't see any indication of him.

Paddy was raised by an Irish father who was a devout Catholic. He would use "the stick" to discipline his children. When we arrived at the farm where he was born and raised, I discovered this. We had plenty of time to explore the farm because everyone was focused on my sister Maureen, the newborn child, which was entirely appropriate. It felt like stepping back in time by a hundred years in some places, as if time had stopped. Farmhouses in the Knockadoon neighbourhood had missing roof slates, deteriorating wooden frames, and loose stone bricks on the walls. I decided to call the neighbourhood "Knock 'em down" rather than "Knockadoon" because, as I glanced down the lane, every house needed work done on it. The farm had the name Clover and was one of around seven on the lane.

When walking through the farmhouse, the hall was similar to the famous shrine at Knock. It was adorned with religious images. The most striking was a small statue of the Virgin Mary with a container of holy water beneath it, which was used to bless yourself. Visitors were greeted by a wall-mounted image of the Pope, giving the impression that he was looking down on them. We were expected to make the sign of the cross in front of a large crucifix or face punishment from whatever adult was present.

The living room was toward the end of the hall. I noticed there was no television set, only a vintage radio on top of an old wooden table with about six chairs from the previous century. The radio reminded me of the same one we had back home, which my mum's family used to crowd around during the war, listening to the BBC to see what area was going to be bombed, as I walked across the bare floorboards. I noticed the kitchen on the left, where there was an old stove in the corner and a sink cluttered with unwashed pots and pans,

The so-called fireplace was near the back of the room, which I assumed was where they spent the majority of their time. It was filled with smouldering, blackened peat debris that they used in place of coal, and a faint odour was wafting through the air.The smell became more overpowering once they successfully started the fire and used it to heat the entire house. I was glancing around the room taking in all the sights and sounds of the place, when an elderly woman, whom I presumed to be my grandmother, suddenly came in. She reminded me of Granny from Beverly Hillbillies, with her old round spectacles, her hair pulled back, waving a walking stick. She was irritated when she discovered me poking around and yelled at me to leave.

As I stepped out the back door, I heard pigs snorting to my right and hens scrambling around my feet looking for corn. In front of us were an old barn and a large field with cows grazing quietly on the grass. Compared to the fog and smoke from the mill chimneys back home, the air seemed incredibly different as I took a breath. My grandmother followed me outside while muttering under her breath about her family from England taking over her wonderful country house. I ignored this and continued to be enthralled by my surroundings.Even though it took me a bit to warm up to my grandmother, she kept saying how much Paddy's younger self reminded her of me. One of my favourite recollections of grandmother is when she called me and led me to an old cowshed made of stone bricks where hens were scurrying around. The outbuilding's wall had a few loose bricks on the floor and had a strange reddish-brown colour. She questioned me, "Which of these hens do you like the most, Michael?" I pointed to the one with the best look, and before I could say anything, she had picked up one of the loose bricks and slammed the hen's head on the brick wall. I will surely be affected by this experience; it truly surprised me. The reddish-brown colour of the wall started to make sense in all its detail. I then realised that our dinner would probably consist of chicken since I wasn't especially hungry at the time.

Later, when I was having fun in the field and talking with the hens to tell them not to be scared and to stay far away from the wall, my grandmother called the children in. "Get in quickly, the tinkers are here, they are coming down the lane, we have to hide," she bellowed. I looked out of the window and could see down the lane where there was a horse-drawn, brightly painted caravan with a very scruffy and dirty man smoking a pipe, accompanied by a young girl with a dirty face, walking alongside it. We were told to hide under the table or anywhere else we could find. Soon after, one of the "Tinkers," as the group of people was known, knocked on the door. The children were completely silent, except for my brother John, whose knees were trembling and tapping on the table's leg. When the Tinker knocked a second time and a third time, there was still silence. My grandmother finally lost patience and yelled, "There's nobody in," to which the man, to my astonishment, replied, "Okay, thank you very much, Mrs.," and left.

I still find it hard to believe his response. It was at this point that I realised how different life was in the West of Ireland than it was in Oldham, I also understood how much of an impact and influence God had on their lives. Someone would yell, "Holy Mary, Mother of God," or "Jesus, Mary, and Joseph," if there was a strong wind blowing through the home or any inclement weather, like a rainstorm. Everywhere you looked, the sign of the cross was being made in every corner of the house.

My mother, who was much more accustomed to it than we were, thought it was funny. She frequently escorted us from the room, prompting me to leave the house before she started laughing. She led us to Irishtown Centre, which consisted of a church, a pub, and a shop with one petrol pump outside. According to my mother, they would attend mass in the morning, drive up to the shop to fill up, buy woodbines from the store, get drunk in the pub, and then drive home. We walked down the lane and the village priest was coming towards us and we all said, "Good morning, Father," as we walked down the lane. As a seven-year-old, having so many fathers—my father Paddy, the father who art in heaven, the holy father in Rome, and even bloody father Christmas was quite confusing. My focus was soon diverted as we continued down the lane by the music coming from the dancers in the tiny village square outside the tavern. a man with a side drum and another one playing the violin. Three young kids were dancing in the manner of the Scottish highlanders I had seen on television at home, despite the fact that their arms were by their sides. When I told Lena about it, she responded, "Their arms are at their sides because a very long time ago, the Catholic church forbade dancing in Ireland, so if someone peered in the window, they appeared motionless." "They simply danced with their legs." Even though I wasn't sure if she was joking, I took her word for it.

As I approached, I noticed one of the children. I recognized the young girl. It was the one who was walking alongside the caravan of the tinker. Lena said, "It must be the only way they survive by begging and dancing as they travel around." We observed them for a while before noticing the church that stood out in the community. It was very modern, with stained-glass windows depicting angels with harps. All the saints and martyrs were inviting us to the heavenly altar. Since the door was always open, Lena decided to answer the saint's call and we entered after being greeted by the scent of incense. I immediately saw a weird environment, with what appeared to be an aura of coloured lights surrounding the altar. Lena laughed and said it was just the sun shining through the stained glass windows, but it was enough for us to find our way out when I added that I thought we must be in the presence of God. I was a little concerned about this. Lena laughed and sprinkled me with holy water from the font at the back of the church as we hastily made our retreat..

.

As we reached the farmhouse after a tour of the so-called town centre, we would be met by the strong scent of peat smoke coming from the chimney and my Uncle Mick leading the cows into the barn for milking. We would return to the house just in time for tea. I could see my grandma and my cousin butchering the chicken I had sentenced to death through the open kitchen door. I was advised to leave the kitchen and wait outside for the call that said dinner was ready, with the thought of eating that poor bird in my mind. My thoughts were interrupted when Paddy came out and led us all inside the house in a manner much like how Uncle Mick led the cows. We all took our seats at the nicely set table and prepared for the grace ritual, in which we gave thanks to God for the meal we were about to eat. I was unable to confront the chicken, but the idea of good hiding off Paddy enabled me to do so.

After dinner, we would gather in the living room, where Paddy would tell us that Grandad would become a Shanakee. At first, I didn't understand what a Shanakee was and assumed he would transform into some sort of monster, but after hearing him explain that it is Gaelic for a storyteller, I began to look forward to it. We all sat down and relaxed on the floor in front of the fire. He began by telling some really nice tales about the Galway community known as Music Fields. My siblings and I were enthralled and believed that everywhere there were crops of trumpets, guitars, and harps instead of plants. Also about a neighbourhood called Fairyhouse near Dublin, which we assumed to be the home of the fairies and elves. In Punchestown, boxers were born, and lions and leopards roamed the streets of Leopardstown. As I went into the kitchen for a sip of water, I overheard Lena, who was laughing to herself while listening to all of this, telling my older brother, "I can see where Paddy gets his passion for horse racing from—these are not towns, they are Irish racecourses." We were getting tired and yawning because the stories were so long until he started telling us about ancient Ireland. He would instil fear in our impressionable minds by describing the banshee's bitter shriek as it soared past the house, which served as a warning that someone was about to perish. Additionally, there were leprechauns, and if you saw one, keep looking at it because if you didn't, either you or it would vanish. This made it difficult for us to sleep at night, especially when my older brother tried to imitate the banshee cry.

Another memory that stuck in my mind, all those years ago, is when we all went to a cemetery in Irishtown to visit my Great Grandfather's grave. All of the graves were together, except for one, which was right in the corner, far away from all the rest. I asked my father why it was on its own, and he told me that it was a nine-year-old boy who was travelling through the town. He went on to tell me that the young boy had died from lung disease and that no antibiotics or medication were given to save him. My father told me that the reason he was on his own was that he was a tinker and that he wasn't allowed to be buried next to the so-called normal people of the community. Whilst they were praying over the grave, I crept away and visited where the boy was buried and managed to say a prayer before Paddy grabbed me by the scruff of the neck and dragged me away, saying, "Don't ever let anyone see you at those people's graves; they will think you are one of them." I still often think about that poor lad on his own and how prejudiced the Irish were against them.

As a seven-year-old, the two weeks I spent in Irishtown were very puzzling because they contrasted greatly with my mother's way of life, which was much more laid back and did not involve worrying about the old man in the sky who was waiting to strike you with a lightning bolt if you did anything improper or neglected to bless yourself during stressful times. Thank God I only had one Irish Catholic parent.

Lena

Madeleine Leech was the real name of Lena. She was raised on a council estate in Oldham after being born on August 6, 1927, as the second youngest of five children. Her father, Tom, who managed to survive World War One, worked as a farmhand, which at the time didn't pay well, especially given the possibility that Germany would be threatening to invade Europe once more and that England would have to prepare for the imminent invasion. It was difficult for him to feed and clothe Lena and her siblings because his wages were severely taxed and products and produce were becoming scarce.

However, when the war started, things were about to get significantly worse. Her older brother, Thomas, who had joined the navy, was severely wounded and stuck in a hospital in Portsmouth. The rest of the family stayed together and managed to survive the rest of the conflict as best they could. Tom was wounded in the first war and developed severe stomach problems as a result of the gas. He tragically passed away in 1941 at the age of 44.

When the war ended, it was difficult to find employment in Oldham because all the surviving soldiers took all the open positions, except for the cotton mills, which were poorly paid and not a very healthy place to work. However, Lena reasoned that working there was better than nothing, so she trained as a ring spinner and worked full-time; this was to be her primary occupation throughout the 1940s and 1950s, even though she detested the work; the camaraderie and kindness of her workmates all pulling together got her through the post-war years. She met Paddy, a smooth-talking Irishman who swept her off her feet, during those years when she was out with her pals. You would have assumed Paddy had lived here all his life while courting Lena. After touring all across Lancashire and Yorkshire and taking her to all the racecourses, they always ended up in the local pubs, which he seemed to know well in addition to the local people in the town.

St. Mary's

We returned to Oldham on a sombre, wet day, and as I made my way up Horsedge Street toward our two up two down terraced home in the shadow of St. Mary's Church, I couldn't help but feel unhappy about having to attend St. Mary's school the next day. As soon as I returned, Lena, as everyone called my mother, took the tin bath down from the wall, and my siblings and I waited to shiver in the kitchen for our turn, the oldest being the first to be bathed. "You have to be clean for school in the morning. "You know what the nuns are like," she added as she scrubbed each of us, reminding us of the notion of going back to the dreadful place. We almost drowned as she dipped our heads in the ice-cold water.

We walked to school in the morning, which was about half a mile down the street. On the left as we walked down was a big old scary house that Lena called the Vicarage. It was the home of the local priest and we could see his silhouette in the window as he watched us approach the big wrought iron gates of the school.

We would usually walk into the line for the regular inspections and a nun would be waiting for us. To check for nits, she would inspect our hands and ruffle our hair. We would get a hit and be hauled to the mother superior if we weren't clean. That old bag was a teddy bear in comparison to Paddy. Fortunately for us, the tin bath usually worked.

As it was very early in my childhood, my memories of those days at St. Mary's are a little hazy, but I do remember the nuns and how they treated the children; I could see the hatred in their eyes as they taught us, looking for any opportunity to give us a crack or a good hiding, and the other kids could see it too, so I was not alone. I knew they were terrified of these people who had devoted their lives to God and often wondered if he knew how they were treating his children. None of the children enjoyed going to school. It reminded me of the workhouse in Oliver Twist. We would always moan to Lena on the way to school about why we had to go, and her response was that if we didn't, I and your dad would go to jail and you would end up in the Scattered Homes. I thought that sounded worse than the Workhouse, so we settled for the nuns. The reason it was a bit hazy was that most of my experience there was not very nice and I blocked a lot of it out of my mind. At one point, Lena had to drag me down the street, every day we would invent some bogus illness trying to prevent us from going.

Game st

When I arrived home from school one day, Paddy was already seated in his chair, chain-smoking the woodbines, a glass of Guinness in his hand, and he was reading a letter with a disturbed expression. He turned to my mother and said, "What are we going to do, Lena? I wasn't expecting this." The letter was a council order for a compulsory purchase order that was part of their plan to demolish the town's older homes. The offer for the property was peanuts, and Oldham council offered Paddy a council house, but Lena, who had spent her entire childhood on an estate, had other ideas. Oldham Council was determined to knock down Saint Mary's Ward in the 1960s to make way for a new housing estate and couldn't care less about the residents. She started house hunting and discovered a three-bedroom house that would cost 2,550 pounds; at the time, this was a significant sum of money, and she knew they would struggle to afford it. The location was called Glodwick, it was next to an old quarry known as "the lows." It was an abandoned quarry that had previously been a coal mine and brickworks. We were all pleased when our mother announced before the transfer that we would be moving to Game Street because the name of the street generated all kinds of possibilities in the playground of our imaginations.

We moved into the new house, which was larger than the small two-bedroom one we had just left. I shared a bedroom with my two brothers, and the girls had what they called the "box room." The house had an inside toilet and a running bath, but there was no central heating, so we had to use a coal fire to heat the entire place. Paddy was thrilled to find a long garden at the back with overgrown weeds and grass. I was aware at the time that he would transform it into a little vegetable farm with potatoes, carrots, and any other form of food that consisted of roots. Aunty Mary the midwife, a frequent visitor, had just returned from her yearly pilgrimage to Lourdes at the time. She'd brought with her a gift that would haunt all of us throughout our adolescence: a picture of Jesus Christ with his piercing eyes following us around and his sacred heart shining brightly surrounded by a crown of thorns. Paddy decided to hang it above the mantelpiece in the back living room.

The front room was hardly used, Lena called it the best room usually for visitors or when the priest called preferably when they wanted us out of the way, it was separated by a petition with glass panels with frosted glass so we couldn't see through and only hear them mumbling, the eyes of our Lord would be watching us, so we never tried to hear or see them anyway, we never got up to any mischief in the back room and Paddy always said the picture was better than any guard dog. We also managed to save a kitten from my grandmother's house before it was drowned which used to happen regularly if your cat had a litter and you couldn't afford to keep them, it was a Tom and we named it Tiddles it was very aggressive and the nastiest animal in the neighbourhood the only person it liked was Paddy, he seemed to have a way with animals, I suppose growing up on a farm in a remote village in the west of Ireland you get to know them, maybe that's where his love of horseracing came from and he loved to pass on his knowledge of it to his sons. While all my friends knew the names of all the footballers by the time I was ten years old, I could read the form on a racecard and Grand National day was like the cup final.

The Bookie

He would frequently go to the bookies on his days off from work, informing Lena he was going to meet his friend "Frank." Lena was trying to do the housework one day when my brother and I started to bother her and she couldn't get her cleaning done. " Take these two with you so I can finish," she said, so we set off to meet Frank. We had to wait outside since Frank didn't like kids, Paddy said as we were walking. When we got to the house, I noticed the sign "Frank Whitehouse, Your Local Bookmakers" over the door. As he opened the door, which was similarly blacked out and had cigarette smoke leaking from it, the house had enormous glass windows painted a dingy cream colour with a gap of clear glass at the top. We could make out a muffled voice that sounded like the speaker at the train station informing you of the arrival times of your trains. John hauled me up on his shoulders because I decided I had to see what was happening inside. I peered through the window gap and saw around six

24

or seven men shouting at a speaker in the top corner of a room and yelling for their dogs or horses to get to the winning post while holding pieces of paper in their hands.

John's strength began to fail, and I was only able to see inside for a little time before I crashed to the ground, bashing the window as I fell. The disturbance caused the bookie to hurry out, he was about twenty stone, with a bald head, glasses, and a large belly hanging over his trousers. He came towards us, calling us brats, and tripped over the doorstep. His barely-fitting pants began to fall as he crashed to the ground. When Paddy came outside to investigate, the bookie was by this point struggling to stand up; he was on his back like a dying fly shaking his hands and legs trying to get up off his back. Paddy hurriedly directed us away from the building. We were prepared for a good hiding when we came home, but instead, he informed Lena that he had never laughed so hard in his life and that the bookie had gotten what was coming to him.

One of my friends' father, who was Paddy's friend and with whom they frequently shared drinks at the neighbourhood pub, caught my attention as I peered through the bookmaker's window. His three children weren't the most fashionable youngsters on the block and frequently got into criminal trouble. Lena felt sorry for them because they often came to see us. She would offer them food or some coppers, depending on what she had in the cupboard or her purse. Lena was aware that their father frequently came home after losing all of his money at the bookies, and I am aware that he had a stable job.

<h2 style="text-align:center">The Barber</h2>

The barber and the dentist were two places I detested going to. Paddy would usually give me a haircut with a basin on my head and a pair of scissors, if I didn't stay very still, he would remove the basin and replace it with the palm of his hand wrapped around my ear. But as I got older, Lena would take my two brothers and me to Harry the Barber on Lees Road. On the outside of the shop, a red and white-striped pole jutted out above the door. Lena explained to us that it represented the bandages and blood of the soldiers in both wars that the barbers used to perform surgery on them as well as cut their hair. This didn't put our minds at rest and we thought maybe the basin cut isn't too bad after all. As I walked in the door there was a long corridor with the sound of scissors snipping away and people talking. The door at the end of the corridor was open and Lena ushered us in. Harry, the barber, was a middle-aged man with glasses who frequently had a full-strength capstan cigarette smoking away from the corner of his mouth. As he clipped someone's hair, he added, "Sit down, I'll be with you shortly." I was dreading having to go first, so I let my brothers go. I observed as he pulled on their heads, twisting them into the proper position, muttering under his breath how he hated cutting kids' hair, but we had lots of practice keeping still with Paddy. If I had an itch on some part of my face from stray hair, I would sneak my hand from under the old towel he put around us and scratch it. Occasionally, he would catch me and whack! His hand would slap against my ear but I preferred the pain of that rather than the itchy feeling. I think he had a disliking for children in general, plus he didn't charge as much as the adults. After we finished, we went to find Lena who was busy in the laundrette next door. We always complained to her about how he treated us. She said "let me have a word with Paddy I know this man drinks in the Brown Cow pub, he will sort him out" he was no match for Paddy and I felt a bit sorry for him, Lena told us he bought Paddy a few pints and told him we were messing about and fidgeting whilst he was trying to do his job. So we got a crack off Paddy and Harry's attitude got worse every time we went.

The Dentist

Toothpaste was a luxury in the bathroom and Lena only bought it now and again, I had never known Paddy to have any teeth, not even false ones. If there was no toothpaste, he would tell us to use salt on the toothbrush. So the inevitable used to happen and we would all end up at the dentist. Nearly all of the kids in Oldham were terrified of the one and only national health dentist, which was located on the side of the bus garage on Gower Street. There were plenty of private ones if you were lucky, but we couldn't even afford toothpaste, let alone a dentist. One day I had a toothache and couldn't stand the pain any longer, so Lena decided to take me after school, when I had my first encounter with this terrible institution. Children were weeping and crying loudly in the waiting area, and there was an odd buzzing sound coming from the room. My turn was about to come. Since I had been experiencing toothache for a few days, I reasoned that they couldn't possibly make it worse.

To my astonishment, both the dentist and her assistant were female. I was asked to sit down after noticing the enormous black chair and the obnoxious clinical odour in the room. I furthermore observed the row of silver gleaming devices with liquid-filled syringes set up at the side of the chair. I hesitated before I sat down. The needle on the end of the large syringe that the dentist was holding, touched my gum as he drew nearer. The nurse gripped my shoulders so I wouldn't move when the needle's sharp point penetrated my mouth as I shifted further back in the chair. I recall yelling inaudibly as the nurse tried to restrain my arms as I screamed to get away. After the needle came out, the vice-like grip in her arms relaxed and I made a dash to the door. The dentist stopped me and wrestled me back into the chair, telling me to calm down. I eventually did and surrendered whilst they took the tooth out, stuffing a rolled up ball of cotton wool on to the hole and telling me to bite on it, which hurt me more than the needle. As I entered the waiting area, embarrassed in front of all the other children awaiting their destiny, my mouth felt like it was on fire. Lena grabbed my hand, soothing me with an embrace, and praised my bravery. I believed that if I were brave, I would have sat down on the chair voluntarily and without being restrained. After a week, when my mouth had begun to heal, Lena brought me an item she had read in the Oldham Chronicle. Oldham's "Gower Street Clinic is notorious and needs to be closed down owing to child abuse and guilty of instilling fear and destroying people's faith in dentists." After that, we never returned to the area, and toothpaste appeared in the bathroom.

St. Anne's

Moving house also meant moving schools. The new one was St. Anne's. I started there in junior one (year 3). On the first day, I noticed there were no nuns but on every teacher's desk, there was a strap that seemed to avert everybody's eyes when they walked in. Each morning started with an assembly conducted by the headmaster, who ruled the school with a rod of iron. After that, we went to our classes and as I walked, I could hear the latecomers and kids who were misbehaving in the ranks receiving their punishment. It initially seemed as though the teachers would have trouble keeping the children under control without the strap, but occasionally it worked the other way, and you would often see the same children in front of the teachers, their hands hardened to the sting of the strap. A lot of these kids had such great learning potential and made something of the knowledge that was available to them but the teachers couldn't recognize it or didn't seem to care.

We also visited St. Anne's Church, which was about two streets from the school. Across the street from the church was a small park that was walled off from the church and seemed like a great place to go if I didn't feel like reading the Bible. Paddy knew we hated going but trusted us to go on our own as he attended the nine o'clock mass while we attended the eleven o'clock.

However, the park attracted my brother and me like a magnet. We could see people leaving the church at the end and we merely mixed with them before returning home. When we arrived one day, he was waiting for us and asked, "Have you been to mass?" In a strong Irish voice. " Ask Billy Murphy's father if we haven't; we walked home with them." We avoided looking into his eyes and he asked, "Okay, what was the gospel about?" He knew we were lying because he was taking off his belt and preparing to give us a good hiding. After the sting of his belt, we had no idea what to do and were unable to sit down for a few days. The next Saturday night, while he was out at the pub, I went into my parents' bedroom in search of an old missal I remembered him reading. I discovered it among his collection of cigars and whiskey, and I memorised passages from the gospel for Sunday's mass and I thought it looked like the park tomorrow. But when he inquired about the mass the following day as we arrived home, he responded, "What was the epistle about?" This time, we could not sit down for a week, so it appeared that the church had prevailed. Around this time, I was also pushed into joining the altar boys by the priest, who frequently visited the school. Father Hourigan was a big, intimidating man with a commanding voice who delivered his sermons without the aid of a microphone. I reasoned that if I didn't do this, I would burn in the darkness of hell for all time, as well as suffer Paddy's anger when he found out because Father Hourigan's sermons to the parish's families were enough to create a fear of God in anyone. I therefore left to help the infamous Horrible Hourigan, as he was affectionately known to the congregation, and I frequently tasted the communion wine when he wasn't present.

I would think of it as a perk of the job, as Paddy would say when he brought half a bag of cement home or a few planks of wood to do his DIY jobs on the new house. When we saw this, my siblings and I would get the hell out of there for fear of being his helpers for the evening rather than playing out.

One Sunday morning, after the eleven o'clock mass, Father Hourigan and Paddy were discussing while he waited for me to clean up the altar. They decided that I may serve on the altar for the half-seven mass before I went to school. As usual, I had no input in the decision. It wasn't all that bad, I thought as I walked the two miles to the church every morning in all kinds of weather with the birds singing and the tomcats and burglars on their way home, I was always up in time Paddy made sure of that, he would walk down to the end of the street with me where he would get picked up by his works van which looked like it hadn't been washed for about six months, blue smoke coming out of the exhaust, muffled talking and cigarette smoke wafting out of the windows from his Irish workmates. I would carry on up the hill and I would be hit with the delightful smell of Hindles bakery, which had a shop at the side known as the penny cake shop. The thought of the cakes kept me going through mass and afterwards, as I must have been the only child out at that time and I had my pick of the freshly baked cakes before I went to school. I would sit outside and eat my well-deserved cake, my reward for putting up with Horrible Hourigan for half an hour. Because my "biscuit money," as Lena used to call it, had been spent on a cake for my breakfast, I had nothing to eat at break time and could only have a third-pint bottle of the free milk that everyone else had. Fortunately, our school provided free meals, so I had food at dinner time.

Both I and my classmate Mick, with whom I formed a lifelong friendship, were always first on the playground. Mick's father ran a greengrocer's shop down Abbey Hills Road, approximately five or six miles away, and used to drop him off on the way to the market. It was usually about half an hour before the rest of the kids arrived. We often thought the teachers lived at the school as we never saw them until the bell rang at nine o'clock, Mick used to say they had a bunker underneath the school where they worked out their plan of attack for the lessons. Even though we were the first students at the school, we were frequently last in line because bullies used to push and shove us to the back to gain brownie points as they grinned at the teachers as they passed by. When the bell rang at nine o'clock, everyone queued up in their line for the class. Unknown to them, we were planning a revenge attack the half-hour before anyone entered the playground. In the evening, Mick filled a few small polythene bags with the most offensive-smelling rotting fruit he could find and put them in the back of his father's van, where he had placed his school bag. At the back of his father's store was an old steel dustbin where he would put all the fruit and vegetables that he couldn't sell or that were going bad. The smelliest rotten fruit Mick could find was packed into a couple of small polythene bags and put in the back of his father's van alongside his schoolbag in the evening. We always had a kickabout in the morning and used our coats or sweaters as goalposts. I wasn't much of a football player and frequently ended up in the goals, but the following day he picked up the fruit in his bag and met me in the playground. as we all put our jumpers down he put the bag next to them. The ball was often kicked over the wall and most of the kids including the bullies would go and retrieve it. Mick and I stayed and smeared the fruit and veg over the bullies coats and bombarded the two of them with the rest. They were taken aback by this and begged for us to stop. The bell rang and the usual scuffling to get to the front began I could see the look on the teacher's faces, holding their noses and wondering what the smell was as we filed past, The two boys who had teased us every morning were the ones she dragged out as we were walking, so I had to hold back my smirk. Needless to say, they kept their distance in the future as they were frog marched weeping to the headmaster's office, and I thought it serves you right.

The school was an old victorian looking place that smelled of disinfectant with varnished floorboards everywhere to stop the children from running or escaping, the teachers dressed very formal in suits and ties and never smiled, our form teacher was called Mr Fitzpatrick he was very tall with a moustache he was ok I suppose but if you crossed him you would taste the strap on your hands with no mercy. His subject was arithmetic, and he often reviewed the timetable and calculations in pounds, shillings, and pence. The classroom was always dismal and confined. I wasn't very interested in the lessons and looked forward to the break, when, barring a severe thunderstorm or blizzard, we had to go outside and avoid the bullies' retaliation. There were two in particular who, for some reason, developed a hatred for me and would follow me, ridiculing and calling me names behind my back. Henry Cooper would have been proud of my right hook when I turned around one day and caught one of them. The boy went to the ground sobbing, and his friend fled to the teacher. When I was taken to the headmaster's office, they pretended that I was the bully and I got my first taste of the dreaded strap on my hands. The headmaster gave me four, and afterwards, I lost feeling in my hands and thought I had gotten worse off Paddy. I refrained from crying and told myself that it was well worth it to keep them off my back. In general, St. Anne's didn't seem like a pleasant place to be during my first years at school, and every day I yearned for the bell to go off at four o'clock.

After School

The walk home was about two miles and was never without incidents along the way, other schools finished their lessons at the same time so we always had shortcuts to avoid the bullying bastards from other schools, who treated us like rival football fans after the match, one of the shortcuts involved running the gauntlet of a few dogs where the owners let them run wild whilst they were at work one of them was the Taylors dog who lived at one of the streets we had to walk down, it was a Jack Russell and had a liking for my brother, as we walked past it would run up to us and start to mount John's leg he would shout at the dog but this seemed to make his grip tighter, John would scream at me "Mick get him off me please get him off" by this time the dog was going like the clappers John had run up the road and didn't stop until he arrived at Game street where Lena was waiting at the doorstep wondering what all the fuss was about. I was on the floor laughing. Eventually, an older woman came out and nearly drowned the dog with a bucket of cold water since I was sitting on the floor too weak with laughter to help him. I eventually stood up and laughed the entire journey home. I could sense how good Lena's cooking smelt as I came closer to the house. With the small sums of money Paddy used to give her and the poor wages she earned working evenings as a ring spinner at the mill, she was able to feed and clothe five of us. Potato hash was one of her favourites, and we ate it frequently—at least three or four times per week.

It was made with potatoes, mince, carrots, and onion gravy and occasionally had a crust on top. When we got home from school, I would always be hungry and ask for something to eat or a few pennies to buy some sweets to pass the time before the long wait until six o'clock when Paddy got home and we were called in for tea. She would say, "There is some bread and sauce in the kitchen. Make do with a sauce butty until your dad gets here." I entered the kitchen and opened a cupboard. It was like Old Mother Hubbard's; the only items in the cupboard were a bottle of HP sauce and a couple of slices of bread. There were always 10 park drive tipped on the table, and Paddy was well-known in the pub, even though I injured my hand by beating the bottom in an attempt to get some out. She didn't have much money, but the one thing she did have was hope, which she generously shared with her children. I sometimes thought, "Hope doesn't buy me a new uniform or put nice food on the table," but we got through the tough times thanks to her positive outlook on life. With our stomachs growling, we would wait at the top of the street, watching for Paddy going up the old cart track on his beat-up bike at the foot of the lows. To avoid becoming Paddy's labourers for the rest of the day helping him with his DIY projects or in the back garden, which was a very long lawn that he had converted into an allotment where he had rows of potato plants and other vegetables he tried to grow, we always quickly finished our plates, mostly out of hunger but also to finish before Paddy and disappear. Paddy couldn't always understand or have the patience to explain what he was trying to tell me, as if he assumed I already knew, such as when I was assisting him in putting down new floorboards in the hall on a day when I couldn't escape and play out. He asked me to saw a piece of wood, first showing me how to use it. I completed the task, and he said, "You are going against the grain, go with the grain." When I tried again, he raised his voice and told me to go with the grain because the plank of wood was breaking up. Finally, he grabbed the saw from me and decided to saw it for himself. If he had explained what the grain was, perhaps he wouldn't have been so frustrated and angry. This happened a lot to my siblings and I, usually when he was doing DIY around the house he couldn't afford to get a Builder or Joiner so he would try to do it himself. Another example was the fence at the bottom the back garden, which consisted of pieces of wood planted in the ground and short planks of wood nailed to them; it reminded me of the fences on the farm in Ireland. They had a modern tall fence next door, with long iron poles covered in strong wire. He used to wonder why he had to replace the fence after it vanished in November; the kids in the neighbourhood were always looking for wood, and it always ended up on the bonfire. Communicating with Paddy was difficult because everything had to be done his way, regardless of whether it was the easier or better way to do something.

Lena, on the other hand, was more relaxed and laid back. When he wasn't around, she let us do our own thing and we could get away with a lot. She'd feel less stressed and sit with a brew and a fag, usually a woodbine she'd gotten from Paddy, and let us run wild in the house while keeping an eye out for Paddy's return. As soon as we saw him, everyone went silent and sat still, as if nothing had happened. He'd sit in his chair, watching the news on the black and white television, and we'd sneak out the back door, one by one, to freedom on the streets.

The Lows

Our favourite playground was the Lows, which was like a miniature mountain range with cliffs and hills. We gave certain locations names, and at the bottom was a small range of what appeared to be blue earth mounds but were remnants of coal that had solidified over time. We called this the blue hills. It was a popular location for bikers. Further down to the left was a flat area that had once been brickwork with half bricks and concrete lying around known as the Brickyard. As you continued down from the Brickyard, you were met with what appeared to be a large crater; On one side, it was full of cinders and shale; this was the red ash. On the side of the red ash, there was what appeared to be a cliff face with rocks jutting out, Goats would climb up this cliff leaving indents where their hooves sank in, it was known as the Goat track. Many of us had been stuck on the track trying to climb up it and had to be rescued by anyone who was walking by or heard our cries for help. When we told Lena we were going out she always said, "don't go on the lows" which often fell on deaf ears as we had no fear but she knew the dangers. At the top of the lows was a fantastic view spanning four counties Lancashire, Derbyshire, Cheshire, and Yorkshire, where around this time the moors murderers Hindley and Brady were still at large, We were constantly warned not to approach strangers by Lena and Paddy, who were perpetually concerned.

John and I were requested to take Paddy's empty bottles to the pub one afternoon during the summer holidays to obtain the penny deposit back on each one; the pub was the Dog and Partridge, which was about two miles away. We arrived at the pub, and as soon as we walked in, one of the customers said, "And who might you two be then?" in an Irish accent. Before we could say anything, the landlord told him, "It's ok, they are Paddy's lads." The landlord took the bottles off of us and started counting the pennies. As we were leaving, the Irishman gave us both a bag of crisps and a bottle of orangeade and said, "It's ok, I am a mate of your dad's." But he was a stranger to us; half a mile up the road, out of sight of the pub; we dumped the orange down a grid, believing it was poison; the crisps ended up on the lows; we decided not to tell Lena about the strange man in the pub, and we handed over the pennies from the bottles. A few days later, when Paddy inquired as to whether we had spoken to anyone in the pub, we replied honestly, out of concern that he might take his belt off. To our amazement, he laughed to himself as he tousled our hair, called us good boys, and gave us each sixpence. Lena took us to one side and said the man's name was McGraw and had known your dad for years but you weren't to know that, you did the right thing by not trusting people you don't know. Oh, and don't spend your money at Ripley's shop because I owe them tick We went down the road to Bob's shop, where he was slow to come out and most of his profits went into the pockets of the neighbourhood school kids who had picked up on this. We bought exceptionally tough liquorice sticks with the money, broke them up, and put the pieces in water-filled, empty milk bottles. The water turned dark after a few days and resembled a beer bottle. The bottles were kept in a cupboard beneath the stairs. The cubby hole was how Lena referred to it. Sometimes we went to get them and only one was there. After a few pints at the neighbourhood pub, I was certain Paddy had confused the Spanish juice, as we used to call it, for a bottle of Guinness. If you didn't want to throw anything away, it went in the "cubby hole," as the phrase goes.

Polly

Our grandmother, who was affectionately referred to as Polly even though her real name was Mary, always had the kettle on, I think that's how she got her nickname. She also had cubby holes throughout each room, which her cats loved to use as hiding spots. When we visited her, one of our tasks was to clean the cubby holes because, due to her arthritis, she was unable to bend down very far. Nothing was thrown away, and whenever we opened the door, we were met with the cat's claws and all of her clutter. "We might need that one day," she would frequently say.

Polly was the typical lovely old lady who loved all her family and couldn't do enough for them, her husband Tom was a first world war veteran who died at the age of forty-one who sadly we never met, Polly told us he had shell shock and suffered from his stomach due to mustard gas, he enlisted in the Manchester Regiment in 1914 at the age of eighteen and met her after the war.

We had a great relationship with our uncles and aunts, and one or two of them were always there when we visited, Lena's only sister was Auntie Doris, whom we nicknamed "chicken leg Doris," because at every party we went to she would always have a chicken leg in one hand and a Benson and Hedges in the other, Doris worked at Park Cake Bakery and wore a hair net that she never took off, and Polly's kitchen was always crammed with Madeira cake, Parkin cake, and Chorley cake. Doris used to call this " mard arse cake." She would get the Chorley Cake out whenever we fell or hurt ourselves, call us a mard arse, give us a piece, and send us back out to play.

Polly loved a bet on the horses, so she got on with Paddy, and he would always put her bets on for her, and he told me she would always be winning but told people she hadn't. If we asked her how did your horse got on her reply every time was "it never got a mention I don't know why I bother." I think she treated Paddy with a few bob to keep him quiet because he always had a smile on his face when he came back from the bookies, Every holiday during the school year, she would come to see us. She would take two buses, go down one of the steep hills leading to Game Street, sit down, and then resume

46

speaking after regaining her breath. We always looked forward to seeing what delights she had packed in her luggage, which was usually empty, so she was sadder than we were that she couldn't afford to bring us anything.

We frequently stayed at Polly's, and she would bring one or two of us back to her home on a council estate called Lime Side. She lived alone with about four or five cats, was well-liked on her street, and received a lot of calls. I would sit in the living room while she was having tea with some of her visitors. When they finished, they would turn their cups upside down, tap the bottom, and give them to Polly, who would look at them and tell them what was going to happen. Lena responded, "She is reading tea leaves, it's a type of fortune-telling, and it's a gift that has been passed down to us," when she noted how captivated I was by this. Paddy warned me not to tell the priest about her because he would have her exorcised if he believed she was the devil. When I glanced into the cup, expecting to see a lot of writing, all I saw was tea. After that, I experienced nightmares for a week.

We enjoyed going to Polly's because there were always things to keep us occupied and she would find us jobs to do, One day she gave us two buckets of old food out of the kitchen and said, "Take them to number thirty-four and he will give you some sweets and a balloon each" I thought this man must be very hungry or very poor, as we got near I heard grunting and saw his house was on the edge of a field with pigs running around and I could see a small farmhouse in the distance. As soon as Polly stated, "I've got to look after the pigs, a joint of one of them will be on our table at Christmas," I immediately thought of the poor chickens in Ireland. When we arrived back, Polly explained to us that he gives the food to the farmer as "pig swill."

Doris and Tilly

The sisters of Polly frequently called while we were there. Doris was a bit of a chatterbox, for some reason, she always talked about doom and gloom and got very emotional. We often heard Tilly shout at her, saying, "Doris, will you shut your scriking gob?" Tilly was a small old lady who was blind as a bat and wore enormous jam jar-bottomed glasses. The cats used to hide when they saw her out of fear that she would step on them.

The Daily Mirror racing pages were spread out on the coffee table, and Polly was trying to predict the winners with a small pencil wedged in her ear. The three of them would constantly strive to set the world right, which would irritate Polly.

The living room was like an Aladdin's cave with ornaments everywhere, belts with ornate brass buckles hanging on the walls, shire horses on the mantelpiece, and pot dogs that she had won on the darts stall at Daisy Nook Fairground, which was usually cleared away when Tilly called, and she'd always remind us about the time she knocked two of her prizes off the table "It took me thirty-six darts at a tuppence a go to win those" Tilly always blamed it on one of the cats, but Polly knew she couldn't even see the cats.

If we were lucky, young Doris, Lena's sister, and Polly would take us to the pit club on Sunday afternoon. The club was located about half a mile up the road from where the Chamber Colliery coal mine once stood. The mine has since collapsed, but the social club is still operational. As we walked in we were greeted with a fog of blue smoke from the cigarettes as soon as Doris had a whiff of this she would light a Benson up and tell us to keep quiet when the bingo started, at the interval she would get up and sing a few songs her favourite which I always remembered was moon river by Andy Williams which she would practice on the way to the club in between puffs of her fags usually ending up in her having a coughing fit. Due to her diabetes, Polly would always drink skol lager. She claimed that it contained no sugar, so she could consume as much as she liked without becoming intoxicated. When she had a few drinks, it was the only time she would speak of her husband, Tom Leech, and the hardships he had endured during the war.

Tom Leech

It was the 3rd of April 1896 when Tom Leech was born, Queen Victoria was on the throne, and Robert Gascoyne was running a coalition government. Tom was the second child of a poor family living in Oldham on Radclyffe Street, on the border of the town centre. The area was called St Mary's Ward and consisted of rows and rows of two up-two-down terraced houses mainly inhabited by mill workers, both his parents worked in the mill and struggled to bring him and his sister up but he survived the hardship and when he left school at the tender age of twelve.

He managed to escape the clutches of the mill owners, got friendly with the local farmer and landed himself a job tending to the animals and general labouring. The farm wasn't that big and was situated on a series of hills and fields called Oldham Edge. Tom worked long hours and it was very strenuous but in his mind, he thought nothing was better than the mill. Whilst he was working he could hear the sound of the soldiers marching coming from the local drill hall down the road and often thought about becoming a soldier. He was eighteen years old when the so-called great war broke out and the first few battles nearly wiped out the British army, posters were appearing all over the town and adverts in the local paper urging young men to join up. He decided to accept the king's shilling and enlist in the Manchester regiment due to peer pressure and the allure of a more exciting life over the tedious, monotonous work on the farm. He remembered the day he enlisted: it was December 3rd, 1914, and as he walked the few hundred yards to the temporary recruiting office at the neighbourhood theatre, it was snowing heavily. He hesitated on the way down and considered delaying his enlistment until after Christmas and going in January, but when he saw the line outside and his friends laughing and joking while waiting for their turn, the idea of returning home quickly vanished, and he went to join them. A person had to be nineteen to join the army. Tom was aware of this, but he wanted to contribute to the war effort, so when the on-duty sergeant asked him his age, he lied like half of his friends and there were no questions raised. Tom passed the medical exam, joined the Manchester regiment, and was instructed to report for training the following Monday. On the way home the thoughts and doubts about what he had done were going through his mind and the worst one was what he was going to tell his parents, his feelings were confirmed when he walked through the door and told his mother who immediately started sobbing 'how could you do this Tom you are my only son" she said repeatedly, he tried to comfort her by saying" its ok mum it won't last long I'll be home before you know it, plus it's treble the money I earn at the farm" his father was a bit more sympathetic and proud that his only son was going to fight for the freedom of his country. In the winter of that year, he was sent for training at Heaton Park on the outskirts of Manchester so in the time he had on leave he would visit his parents at every opportunity. At the end of January 1915 he left with his company across the channel to fight in the trenches which would change his life forever, like all his mates he was full of youthful courage and excitement but after a few months of dodging bullets, shrapnel and the deafening noise from the constant bombardment of the artillery he longed to be back on the peaceful farm tending to the animals and his home comforts, his battalion was sent to Ypres in Belgium were he copped for a stray bullet which went through his thigh missing his bone but still it was severe. He was sent back home to recover in one of the military hospitals in the south, the army was losing a lot of men, and officers would patrol the wards and question the doctors and nurses to see if the soldiers were not faking their injuries, and when he eventually left the hospital, he was declared fit and well and sent back to join his unit. It was May 1916 when he arrived in France and joined his comrades to prepare for the big push, and on June 1, 1916, Tom went over the top at the Battle of the Somme. Which claimed around 300,000 British troops, he somehow survived the battle and managed to reach the end of the war physically unharmed, with only a scar on his leg where the bullet went through, but the mental scars were much deeper and he suffered terribly with shell shock, which we now know is a form of PTSD. He, like many soldiers at the time, never talked about what he went through or the horrors he saw or heard that aggravated his situation. He was eventually admitted to a hospital and was recovering in a Strinesdale convalescent home, where he met Polly, who was working part-time in the kitchen.

The Avenues

We usually got home from Pollys just in time for when Paddy went upstairs to sleep after his lunchtime session in the pub, we all used to creep around for fear of waking him up we would get some warning from Lena when he did, which was our signal to get out of the house especially if it was us who disturbed him. The street had plenty of places to hide it consisted of three houses on our side and a row of terraced houses across the road, ours was the middle one of the three, and on the left was a nice family who had three children who we more or less grew up with but to our right was a couple from Poland whom Paddy took a dislike to. Mainly because if our football went over their fence they would either pop it or keep it which was very often, it all came to stop one day when I came home from school Paddy was not working and on my way down I could hear him shouting and swearing to come from the backyard it shocked me because he never swore in front of us, I ran through the ginnel what separated the bottom of the houses just in time to see Lena pulling him off the next door neighbour. Luckily he didn't hit him but the yard was full of balls of all different sizes he had been storing them up in his coal shed Paddy found out and had a go at him, after all, he had paid for the footballs. During the summer, the avenues, as we called them, were constantly crowded with kids playing football and other games and generally getting into mischief. Both Clifton Avenue, which was to the left of the street farther down, and Clifton Close, which was at the bottom, were home to numerous families just like ours. Paddy would decide whether or not to allow us to play with other children, either his pals from the pub or the parents' children who went to church. Every time there was any trouble, even when the offender was unknown, it was always the same families—usually the poorer ones, and yes, we did fall into that category in some ways that received the blame.

There were a lot of characters on "the avenues," such as the man at number one who always blamed my older brother when someone knocked on his door and who would chase

Patrick up the street while yelling, "Get back here you little bugger"; however, he had no chance of catching our Pat because he was like a whippet, and poor old Ernie, who resided at number 19, had rickets and was constantly accosted by bystanders who yelled, "Have you lost your horse, mister?" Also Tommy One Tooth, who lived around the corner from Platts the Butchers and would wander around the streets collecting rubbish, was one person we didn't play about with. The bins had to be outside your home for the garbage men to come, so he would have a good route in them. He would get crazy and start throwing trash at the kids who taunted him, especially old tins or anything that might injure them. He typically got his comeuppance from the parents, which is probably why he only had one tooth.

Mr Platt the butcher was a big fat old man who hated kids going in his shop he wore an old-fashioned hearing aid and was always saying "eh" or "pardon" whilst he was talking to you sometimes I would come home with lamb when Lena wanted ham through him mishearing me, every time we went out of his shop we would say in a quiet voice "see you Mister pratt " his response was usually "what did you say" to which we replied a bit louder "see you mister Platt ``one day his wife was listening and told Lena and we begged her not to tell Paddy she agreed not to and we were good as gold for her for a couple of weeks. Paddy was in and out of work in those days and it was always a case of the feast today famine tomorrow from what I can remember the famine was a bigger percentage.

Aunty Mary

We used to take it in turns to visit Paddy's sister Aunty Mary at weekends usually when he was out of work, she was a very kind hardworking lady and always made sure Paddy had enough food in the house when he was unemployed when we arrived there, she would have a list of chores ready for us to do such as polishing the furniture or going errands she would put all her loose change in big bells whiskey bottles and save it up for us by the way of paying for the jobs we did, her husband Uncle Tommy was usually sat in the lounge watching whatever sport was on the telly. Uncle Tommy always had a crate of Guinness by his side, and whenever Aunt Mary wasn't looking, he would offer us a sip from one of his bottles. On one particular day, after I had completed the usual chores and

Aunt Mary had been called away for an emergency, Uncle Tommy appeared to be a little more inebriated than usual, he asked me, "Do you have any money?" To which I answered, "just my bus fare home."He then started shaking the Bells whiskey bottles and gave me the majority of the silver pieces while saying, "Don't worry, she won't notice," I had a lot of coins when I left, so I chose to spend part of the money on a pick-and-mix to eat on the way home and loads of stamps to add to my collection at Woolworths in the town centre. Aunty Mary's blue Austin A40 could be seen outside the house as I walked up Game Street. When Paddy called me inside, I had the impression that I was sitting in a courtroom with Lena and Paddy serving as the jury, Aunt Mary serving as the prosecution, and the image of Jesus looking down at me serving as the judge.

Uncle Tommy couldn't remember handing me the money from the bottles when he was awakened from his drunken state when she got home, so he assumed I had stolen it. Naturally, I protested my innocence, but to no use. I received a good hiding from Paddy and was forbidden from seeing Aunty Mary's again; the belt stung, but it was worth it not trudging down to her house at the weekend again. We used to be able to tell when.

Paddy's other sisters were coming because pictures of the Madonna and the Sacred Heart would be placed on the mantelpiece beneath Jesus, and Paddy would have his rosary beads clicking on his hands. Paddy's other sisters lived in London and used to visit about once a year, usually for weddings, funerals, or special occasions. His only brother Mick looked after the farm in Ireland. They would all congregate in the living room whilst the men went to the pub I walked in once when I got back from the altar I had a cold at the time and I was coughing and spluttering, they were sat in a circle so they could see each other whilst they were gossiping, their names were Sheila, Annie, Bridie, Sally and Mary and as I looked at them I suddenly felt sorry for Paddy who was very rare and thought no wonder he treats us like he does growing up with this lot prattling on in their Irish accents and signs of the cross every two minutes.

Put your hand over your mouth when you cough or you'll be giving us all the consumption, Aunt Annie interrupted my train of thought. I had no idea what she was referring to but later learned that it was tuberculosis, which was widespread in Ireland in the 1940s and 1950s. I wondered if that was the cause of death for the unfortunate tinker boy buried alone in Ireland. I had only been there for two minutes when Aunt Sally said, "Here's our Michael, he's going to be a priest aren't you?" I simply nodded, but in my head, I was saying, "I don't think so, ladies," and I quickly left the room to join my friends on the street.

The families on the avenue and the close always seemed to have more money, smarter clothes and cars outside their houses. My time at St Anne's was coming to a close and senior school was looming. I was going to St Alban's and I remember Lena struggling to afford my uniform but she managed to get an evening shift as a spinner at the Lily mill which meant Paddy making the tea he was the worst cook in England. Coming from Ireland, he would force us to eat potatoes at every meal, even though they were invariably overcooked and quite hard. Lena used to work in the mill primarily when Paddy was on short notice or when there was no work being done on the construction sites or the roads. Paddy would often be in his worst moods during these times because, as a proud worker, he would become irritated and frustrated at not being able to support his family. This is when his and Lena's arguments became a little heated, and he took most of it out on us, but she was having none of it and always took our side. I remember one Sunday evening when he came home from the pub and fell asleep in the chair; we were all inside due to the rain and being a little noisy, which inevitably woke him up; he was ranting and raving, but Lena stood firm and told him to leave as he slammed the door behind him." Michael, follow him," she said. I hurried out, put on my coat, and barely saw him disappear down Roundthorn Road. I felt like a detective as I followed him to Mumps railway station, which was closed on a Sunday. He rattled the big lock on the gate, muttered something, and set off back to Game Street, with me following him. Lena inquired as to where he had gone. When I told her, she said he was returning to Ireland; When the arguments got worse in the coming weeks, we wished that station was open.

St Albans

The summer holidays were coming to an end and the atmosphere in the house wasn't good, so I began looking forward to the seniors, but stories and rumours were going around about my new school and how awful it was and that the teachers were worse than the old school, so I was a little nervous about going, but Lena always said: "I don't know what you're worried about." "Your school days are the happiest of your life." I wondered what the rest of the days would be like if these were the best. To get there, we had to go up the lows and down the other side, which was a nightmare in the winter, especially when it snowed. During the holidays and weekends, it attracted a lot of kids and families with sledges. We had to do with an old bonnet cover off one of the old cars we found from one of the old asbestos roof garages that were scattered around the bottom of the lows. In the winter the snow would appear to be never-ending. Every year we would seem to have blizzards and deep snow where the wind would cause huge drifts, making it difficult to walk. But it was fantastic for snowball fights, and there were snowmen in everyone's gardens. We built them with Paddy's socks as gloves, which he always found out about, which again led to good hiding, plus we dressed them in his cap and scarf. As a result, our hands were like blocks of ice.

I started school at St. Alban's in 1968. I recall that two years had passed since England had won the world cup, and Polly had taken John and me to the world cup exhibition in Manchester right before the start of the summer.

I was amazed by how crowded and hurriedly everyone was rushing when we left the train at Victoria station. Polly was struggling to keep up as we walked up Corporation Street and turned left towards Piccadilly. As we approached Piccadilly Gardens, I was met with the noise of the big city mixed with hundreds of starlings in the trees that surrounded the gardens. The buildings seemed so high and compact; I felt as though I was in a different world. The rain started to get heavier as we approached the museum, and the person taking our tickets was a proper Mancunian, As he took them off us he had a half-eaten Garibaldi biscuit in his hand and on the side was a mug of tea which he picked up and amongst his slurping muttered: "Welcome to the rainy city".

We walked around the room with a picture of the toothless Nobby Stiles dancing with the world cup in his hand with the rest of his teammates standing out from the wall amongst the glass-fronted tables full of medals and football paraphernalia. Polly sat at a table, talking to the security guard who had made her a cup of tea and shared his Garibaldis with her, as raindrops bounced off the window behind her. It was a little boring after half an hour of wandering around, but we made sure Polly knew we enjoyed every minute of it. My older brother Patrick was a footballer, and John and I were into rugby league, but we didn't tell her, and a day away from Paddy and Oldham with a chance to be in the big rainy city took the sting out of the prospect of St Albans.

Going to this big school and meeting new friends in my school uniform, which was the only one I had and didn't realise had to last me the entire term, made me feel excited and a little grown up. I soon realised the rumours were true when I was placed in a class of about thirty students who had come from various Catholic primary schools throughout the town. As the register was read out, I noticed that all of the names were either Irish, Ukrainian, or Polish; there didn't appear to be any English names.

Even though 90% of the teachers had English names, and the majority of the teachers could handle us, one sign of weakness from them and the class went insane, especially when we had a student-teacher, the kids in the back destroyed them and often reduced them to tears. Mr Taylor was our form teacher, and he had a twitch in his eyes when he spoke to us. We found it difficult not to laugh, and if we did, we were sent out to wait for the strap, which, like my former school, was never far from his side. He was known to all of the school as Colonel Blink, and he was a good teacher if you didn't look him in the eyes for fear of bursting out in laughter, He also had a great aim with chalk and the board duster, and a few of us went home with souvenirs on our bodies from his ranting. Health and safety were non-existent, bullying lurked in every corner of the school, and at the back of the school, hidden away from the teacher's gaze, was the infamous smoker's wall; smoking was a four-of-the-strap offence, so about ten yards away from the wall would be a couple of first-year students reluctantly recruited by the bullies to act as lookouts. The poorer kids were given five dinner tickets for free school dinners at the start of each week; they were similar to blue raffle tickets and became the local currency, on a Monday morning, being traded for fags or money, luckily our house wasn't that far away and with an hour for dinner time, I could sneak in and make something to eat while making a few bobs on the tickets where there was usually plenty of buyers from the kids who had been given money to buy their meals. I became accustomed to seeing lines of misbehaving students outside the headmaster's office during my first two years at the school. The teachers ruled the school with an iron fist in a harsh and often cruel manner. But I thought this was nothing compared to Paddy's wrath; my only concern was that he would find out about our bad behaviour. The groups of kids formed their social circles depending on where they came from or how smart or scruffy they were, and the teachers had their favourites from the start. I didn't fit into any of those categories.

My circle of friends was always in trouble, and trouble seemed to follow us everywhere, and the favourites would make sure the teachers knew about it. For example, when I accidentally broke a window in the boy's toilets, I was summoned to the deputy headmaster's office and accused of punching the window for no reason. What occurred was that as Mick and I were pretending to fight, I accidentally broke a window with my elbow, scattering glass all over the ground. Naturally, we ran away, but unbeknownst to us, a first-year pupil recognised our voices from one of the cubicles. Mick was taken into the headmaster's office while I was in the deputy head's office. before we went in we sorted our story out together and said whatever they say stick to our version, it was around nine-thirty when the interrogation started with two of them questioning me they tried all sorts of ways to get me to admit to the crime and after about two hours of this came their master stroke, one of the teachers who was drilling Mick came in and said, "You might as well admit it he has told us everything and said you did it" I thought the games up and reluctantly admitted to punching the window even though I didn't do it, I saw Mick in the playground later and he said he stuck to the story and didn't say another word I thought this was a valuable lesson to learn and not to trust the bastards. I had to tell Lena about my punishment because she wasn't happy, but she wouldn't tell Paddy and she would intercept the letter because if he found out, my life wouldn't be worth living. I received six of the strap and three of the cane in addition to a letter sent home. In those first two years, I don't think I enjoyed a single lesson, which is probably why I got into so much trouble.

The thought of spending another seven hours learning about the ways of the world from middle-aged men and women made me enter St. Albans very slowly one morning. catching me out on even the smallest mistake and correcting me, usually with a lecture about how I wasn't paying attention and would have gotten it right if I was. My mother's remarks, which kept resonating in my head, that my school days were the finest days of my life, were usually the last thing on my mind as I tried to find out where I was going wrong—which, at the time and throughout my schooling, they most surely weren't. The students were nothing more to any of the teachers than a wage at the end of the week. During a break, I overheard two of them talking to each other as I passed by. The conversation surprised me a little and made me think that they probably dread going to school just as much as I do. The way they talked about the kids—"the dregs of humanity will soon be on their holidays" and "I'll make sure the good for nothings have plenty of homework tonight"—made me feel more incompetent and gave me less hope that I would leave this place with even the barest resemblance of an education.

Some of the teachers even strolled around with the strap over their shoulders ready to give it promptly at any misbehaviour. The teachers were more like prison guards. Many of them appeared to appreciate it. Although I felt that what was happening was wrong, I was helpless to change it. The teachers in this school capitalised on the widespread fear among the students. I decided at that time to keep as low a profile as I could for the few years I had to put up with these vile, cruel people's abuse while I waited for my good friend karma to handle it.

I wondered whilst looking out of the window with the view of Abbey Hills council estate and the faint sound of the ice cream van stopping outside the houses, thinking what was I doing here, also what was he doing there, 'the kids are in school unless all the parents have a sweet tooth you are wasting your time maybe we felt the same.

I couldn't stop thinking about my first days at the school as I daydreamed by the window. You were assigned to a class that matched your IQ based on the results of your junior high school exams. I was placed in the 1LF form. Latin was represented by the L, and French by the F. A dead language, Latin. Only priests are taught Latin, and they only use it when praying. Why then do they waste our time on something I will never use? 1LG Latin and German was the other class. 1F and 1G, who were at the bottom of the pecking order, had the benefit of not having to learn Latin. Lower still was 1B in this form they didn't learn any languages. The pupils in this class mainly had learning disabilities or were dyslexic, But the teachers 'and some of the senior pupils' called this the thick class. I noticed some of the disruptive pupils were given a prefects badge which was a good idea by the teachers. It gave them a sense of responsibility and made them worth something. In addition to keeping them out of trouble for a while until the teachers discovered them allowing their friends to get away with stuff, I could see their self-esteem rising. After that, it was back in the disarray and down to the ground.

Certain activities and events seemed to start secretly with only a select group of pupils, such as drama lessons and specialised events which happened in the school after class. I found this out when the pupils who were picked out for one of the drama clubs put on a Christmas play. I was interested in acting but neither I nor my classmates were invited to take part, again it was the clique of the teachers' pets who were approached to take part. This was happening all through the school terms, and many talented students missed opportunities to make use of the capabilities they had.

Without any assistance from the teachers to pass the time, I spent the majority of the day daydreaming while staring out the window. All I could think about was the long hike across the lows and freedom. Our rival protestant school, Breeze Hill, was on the other side of the lows, and they were dismissed fifteen minutes later than we were out of concern for the frequent school fights that had occurred in the past. To keep yourself safe, if you were in detention you were supposed to walk around the lows by St. Mark's church. However, one day I forgot and started up the lows when suddenly there was a lot of noise and I felt like Michael Caine in Zulu as all the students appeared at the top of the hill. I believe I broke the four-minute mile record as I ran like the wind towards St. Mark's spire. Even on the walk home from school, there seemed to be a danger, but at that age, you didn't realise it or weren't conscious of it.

Smoking

We called this area of the hill "the dark side" and it was perfect for a cigarette on the walk home because it was out of the way of the school and far enough away from Game Street. Most of the young people I knew always had a cigarette in their hands, and they constantly encouraged me to do the same, which I eventually did. That was it, I was addicted to the dreaded weed. I used to enjoy that number six on the way home, munching polo mints by the handful so Lena or Paddy couldn't smell it. I recall almost passing out after the first drag but persisted in trying to be hard in front of them, which was my downfall. Both Paddy and Lena smoked so usually we got away with it. When Paddy's sisters went to Ireland they always brought him gifts back and he would hide them away from us in the bedroom but being the age we were we would have a good hunt around for them and always found his stash. For some reason, you couldn't buy them here. The cigarettes came in packs of fifty, always with one left unopened, and were packaged in a white packet called Sweet Afton, named after a river in Scotland. I always suspected Lena had stolen a few cigarettes, so I took two knowing he wouldn't notice. I smoked them on the dark side of the lows, and to this day, I have never tasted a better cigarette.

At this point, Paddy appeared to be less eager to leave the house than in the past and appeared to watch the news frequently. Additionally, he didn't immediately turn to the racing pages when the newspaper was delivered. I asked Lena what was wrong. She claimed that he is concerned about the unrest in Ireland. To defuse the situation, the British dispatched troops in 1969 when the IRA were making their presence felt in Northern Ireland.. Paddy was a little paranoid and believed the English residents of the town would turn against the Irish population. I don't recall it being all that bad, but he used to be particularly offended by Irish jokes that said they lagged in education, and whenever one was told on a show he was watching, he would become irritated and hurl the television's plug across the room. Because of this, my siblings and I had to leave the house until dad calmed down because otherwise, he would take it out on us.

The paper round

It was the start of the 1970s. I was able to get a paper round at Spencer's shop on Nugget Street so I wouldn't have to serve at the altar during the half-seven mass at St. Anne's, and Ted Heath had just won the general election with a right-wing Conservative Government. Although England had just lost to Germany and eliminated us from the world cup, things weren't too bad. Even if it required waking up earlier than usual in all kinds of weather, there was a payoff at the end of the week.

73

My pay for delivering roughly eighty papers in all types of weather was eighteen shillings. Around six in the morning, when I would stroll down to the shop, the streets were empty but for the occasional early riser coughing on his first cigarette of the day. Additionally, I could hear the buzz and rattle of empty milk bottles coming from my usual milkman, who always wished me a good morning and occasionally gave me a ride on the back of his float as it travelled down Roundthorn Road. Depending on the weather, the owners would greet me when I arrived at the shop a few minutes after six and offer me an orange juice or a hot cup of coffee, and wait for them to mark the papers with the house number and street and then off I would go with this heavy canvas bag stuffed with tabloids and two broadsheets for the posh semi-detached houses down brook lane miles away from the working class terraced houses what most of my round consisted of, as I went round I would imagine what type of person lived in the house by the paper or magazine I delivered. I assumed they were bankers and lawyers because the semi had both a Financial Times and next door a Daily Telegraph, but I was always mistaken as I discovered one morning when I was running late and they were leaving for work; one drove off in a builders van and the other almost ran me over with his ice cream van. It was then very dark and eerie, and I frequently felt like someone was following me down the dark, deserted streets. I expect it was an old tom cat on its way home hoping I would open a bottle of milk on one of the doorsteps which I sometimes did and add it to my list of sins for the confessional box of horrible Hourigan, it was very different to the evening round which was full of life and not as lonely kids were playing in the street and people coming home from their daily toil they would often wait at the door for me to give them there Oldham Chronicle or Manchester Evening News.

The men would go right to the back page for the football or racing results, while the women would go straight to the obituary, and read it on the doorstep before anyone else got their hands on it. After a few months, I began to appreciate the solitude and quiet of the mornings as I watched the lights turn on as people began to awaken, whistling along with the early chorus of birds and attempting to encourage them to mimic my tune. It served as a deterrent from the feeling that someone was following me, and the steeple of St. Mark's did not help either because it resembled a Ku Klux Klan hat in the background, and the clocks that stood in for eyes looked at me like the image of Jesus on our mantlepiece. Nevertheless, it did speed up my round, especially when lightning was flashing all around. I was walking through the morning streets.

In the summertime the air was so crisp and fresh and occasionally I caught a faint smell of peat from the moors where the random grass fire starters had been at work it reminded me of the old fire back in Ireland and I thought it must make Paddy feel a bit homesick if he caught a whiff of it, halfway through my round I would take a short cut up Glodwick road which had a row of shops which at that time in the morning were all closed except for the fruit and veg shop at the corner of Pitt street it was like an old shed adjoining a sweet shop and the locals used to call it the wooden hut, all the fruit was outside on makeshift little stalls there was never anyone around when I walked past so my breakfast was usually an Apple and Orange and I added it to the confession list which by now was getting bigger by the day and I was sure anytime now I would get a lightning bolt or burn eternally in hell but a few Hail Marys and an Our Father would put my mind to rest and ease the guilt I felt from my

Catholic upbringing. The one thought in my mind that I always tried to forget as I walked those streets was going over the lows back to the daily boredom of Albans and the teachers who didn't give a toss about us.

It was now 1971 Ted Heath was still prime minister and was making a right balls of it, Thatcher who was something to do with education had stopped the free school milk there were strikes everywhere, a three-day week and Paddy couldn't get work anywhere, I was walking up the street with Lena one evening it was just going dark and I saw the outline of a man who seemed to be digging on the side of the lows, I said to her "look at that man mum he is digging for gold" her reply was "that's your dad Michael we have no coal for the fire because of the strikes" It was also a year of confusion over the decimal currency which was introduced, all of a sudden all the price of things seemed to go up and most of the arguments between my parents were about money or lack of it. I constantly gave it some thinking. What a waste of time it was to battle with pounds, shillings, and pence figures in school; now we have to start from scratch. As I entered my third year, I was surprised to find that things were becoming a little easier. The teachers had begun communicating with us more frequently and paying attention to our difficulties since they were aware that we were growing older and that our bodies and minds were changing.

They started talking to us a lot more and listening to our problems. We were all teenagers now and a bit more rebellious and more volatile. I told Lena about how they had changed and she said" they are preparing you for adulthood" to be honest I thought they were shit scared of us. But they still had their favourites and the pupils still formed their cliques and groups depending on how wealthy their parents were.

Back to Ireland

In 1971, I returned home from school on the final day of classes before the start of the summer holidays. I noticed my Aunt Mary's familiar blue Austin A40 parked outside the house as I was running down the lows, relieved that I wouldn't have to see the teachers' miserable faces for another six weeks. I hurried into the house out of panic thinking something was wrong. As I entered, Lena was drinking tea with her at the table and smiling at me. "Make yourself a brew and sit with us Michael we have something to ask you" I sat down and started to sip my tea. There was a bit of a pause and Aunty Mary asked me if I would like to go to Ireland with her just for a week, she had asked Pat and Christine, but they went a couple of years ago and said it was my turn, I went silent for a few minutes and thought it would be nice to go on my own without the threat of Paddy watching over me so I agreed.

I learned the day before the trip that we would be travelling from Manchester to Shannon Airport in Galway, so it would be wise to spend the previous night with my aunt. Uncle Tommy was drinking Guinness when I arrived at her house with my old brown suitcase and said, "Get used to it, this is all they drink over there," as usual. I could see he was growing more inebriated as the night went on. Aunty Mary was cleaning up while also ensuring that he had enough food and alcohol to last him the entire week. She sat down and began to explain to me why we were visiting and what the plan for the week would be. She and Paddy had saved up money to purchase a new barn because Grandad wasn't doing well and the farm was losing money. This astonished me because, according to Lena, we barely had enough money for food and clothing. Later, I learned that it was only her money that was providing the funding. As she spoke about Ireland and her family, how they battled to live during her childhood, and as we sat there, I could see her eyes filling with tears, praising herself when she recalled some disappointment. I began to feel bad for her and pondered maybe this is the reason Paddy is the way he is. We decided to end the night and prepare for the following day because Uncle Tommy was becoming a drunker. I didn't get much sleep since I was a little anxious about travelling, especially when he said, "Goodnight, have a wonderful week, and I hope your plane doesn't crash."

The following morning, Aunty Mary's scurrying around to make sure everything was tidy before we left awakened me up. My uncle's snoring could be heard as we left the house while she said a couple of Hail Marys and the taxi arrived on time. We finally got on the plane, and she prayed with her eyes closed, never taking her hands off the rosary beads. Although I was more anxious than she was, all I got from her when I tried to speak to her was in the middle of the prayer. I said a few Hail Marys and thanked God for getting us there safely because I was so happy when the wheels touched down on the runway.

Since Shannon Airport is much smaller than Manchester's, we passed through there quickly. A woman was furiously waving at us as we passed by. I briefly believed it to be Aunty Mary's twin, but it turned out to be her sister Sally who had come to meet us. We hurried into her car and began the drive to Irishtown, interrupting their never-ending chat only to make the sign of the cross whenever we passed a church or a cemetery. The holy family church was waiting for us at the Irishtown crossroads, its stained-glass windows adorned with angels and saints calling everyone inside. The priest was standing at the door, Aunty Sally had the window open, and she was shouting, "God bless you father," which was being echoed by Aunty Mary, who wanted a share of the grace. The odour of burning peat filled the car as we travelled along the lane to Knockadoon which had not been demolished. They both inhaled deeply, and I silently observed that they are aware they are at home.

We were greeted at the door by my grandmother who nearly choked me by hugging me so tight and led us in the hallway doing the ritual of blessing ourselves and genuflecting on the holy pictures and statues. Grandad was sat in the chair he shook my hand with a vice-like grip and Aunty Mary asked about his health he said "I think I'm over the worst, Mick has been doing all the work" which brought a wry smile to Aunty Marys face thinking they had brought her here under pretences.

I could see his stick at the side of him and I thought about the warning Paddy had said and how he was brought up with it, The three women were cackling away talking about Oldham and Paddy making their way into the kitchen, I didn't want to be left alone with him so I thought I,d sneak out the back and see if there were any chickens left what they hadn't eaten. They were now foraging in greater numbers, much to my amazement. Nothing had changed in the farmyard except for the old wooden barn, which had collapsed around an old tractor and was covered in hay. My birthplace was Oldham, so I was a little confused when Uncle Mick beckoned me over while he was busy with the cows, greeted me, and expressed his happiness that I had returned home.

I decided to take a stroll up to where the cows were grazing. An elderly donkey was standing next to them in the field. I nervously approached him holding some grass in my hand to gain his trust. He munched on the grass as I gently stroked his mane.

All of sudden he started to kick his back legs, luckily he didn't catch me with them, in the corner of my eye I could see a young lad of about my age, at the fence giggling to himself and I realised he had thrown a stone at his back which startled him and made him jump. I confronted the lad asking him what he was doing. He was speaking to me, but I was unable to understand a word of what he was saying until I realised that he was speaking Gaelic. About 200 yards behind him, I could see an old caravan with smoke coming from the chimney and a couple of vicious dogs barking near the door; this caravan resembled the one that had called at the farmhouse six years earlier. Aunty Mary had warned me not to approach tinkers if I saw any before I left the house because they might kidnap me. I ran like the wind back to the field where uncle Mick was rounding up the cows because I felt like a cowboy surrounded by Indians. I began to question him about the tinkers, including what they were all about, where they had come from, and why everyone despised them.

He took a seat on the vintage wooden milking stool and began to tell me about the time when English landowners controlled all the farms. Particularly during the potato famine, several farmers who were genuinely struggling couldn't afford to make rent payments. so that the landlords would force them out. Apart from the clothes on their backs, they were left on the street with nothing. They had no other option except to beg. Over the years, with the assistance of some sympathetic farmers, they constructed caravans and trailers and begged for enough money to purchase an old horse or donkey to pull the caravan. Wherever they went they were not allowed to settle, so they travelled the lanes and roads of Ireland begging and selling homemade goods such as lucky charms and trinkets to whoever they met on the way. As he was relating all this to me I thought they are not the awful people my relations were describing to me but they are the same as us, through no fault of their own just down on their luck trying to survive. We all sat down for dinner and said the customary prayers and Grace of thanking God for our food. I then decided that the next day I would go in search of the Tinkers, but this time I wouldn't run but instead try to become friends with them.

The following morning, I discovered Uncle Mick was lighting the fire when I awoke early to the aroma of burning peat. He was sitting in front of the fire with a cup of hot coffee when I decided to get up and join him. I was sneaking about when he saw me and remarked, "Oh, you've decided to help me with the cows then. Although it wasn't my aim, I complied. He gave me a cup of coffee and then began to ramble on about the cows, describing how each one had a name and how they behaved when he approached them. He talked about the cows as though they were people and kept calling them his family.

After we finished our coffee, he went into the kitchen and as I stared at the old fireplace alight with the logs of smouldering peat, I could hear the sizzling noise of bacon frying in the pan, after a while he appeared with a tray full of eggs and bacon saying "get this down you and we'll disappear, the smell is bound to wake the rest of them up".We quickly ate breakfast and as we made our way to the barn I quickly put the leftovers of the bacon in my pocket and I could hear the others waking up to the great aroma of the Irish bacon teasing their noses.

As we got closer to the old barn, Uncle Mick was milking the cows as he always did. I moved toward the coop for the hens. Fortunately, they had been laying, so I put two eggs in my pocket and told Uncle Mick I was going for a walk to check on the donkey in the top field to see if he was well, hoping the tinkers hadn't left. I hesitantly moved towards the top field, holding the leftover bacon in my hand in case the dogs saw me coming. I could see the wisps of smoke from the caravan swirling towards the sky. When I hopped on the fence, the two dogs showed up as expected. I hurled the bacon in their direction while remaining firm. They tore into it as if they hadn't eaten in weeks, forcing me to scramble back over the fence afraid I could be the next victim. The young boy who had thrown the stone at the donkey suddenly appeared and was attempting to push the dogs away from the fence. I greeted him and informed him that I had given his dog,s breakfast. I offered him the eggs, which fortunately weren't broken. The dogs calmed down as he removed them from me and he grinned. He began speaking to me in English, but his Irish accent was considerably thicker than that of my family, and he spoke much more quickly, so I only caught a few of his words. Don't worry about the dogs, he assured me, as they have been trained not to jump or scale fences for fear of being shot by farmers. For me to grasp what he was saying, I had to beg him to speak more slowly.

As I was telling him who I was and what I was doing, he started laughing and said my accent was weird and he had never heard it before. I managed to catch a few words as the boy waffled on without pausing to regain his breath. The dogs by this point had settled down and were snuffling around the grass while he was talking about his family and why they were here. The dogs started barking and the boy was pointing behind me all of a sudden. Uncle Mick was strolling up the field when I turned to look around. The dogs chased after the boy as he ran down the hill. I yelled, "I'll see you here tomorrow," as he raised his palm in an apparent approval gesture.

As Uncle Mick drew nearer, I thought about Paddy as he prepared to give me a good hiding. However, he was grinning as he approached and stated, "You should have said I knew what you were up to." During our chat, I advised him that at home, we had to keep things secret from Paddy and not tell him the truth so that he wouldn't take off his belt and discipline us. He asserted that speaking the truth is always preferable, even if it causes the world to crumble around you. I reacted by saying, "I can understand that, but that's exactly how it feels when I get a walloping from your brother." I began to appreciate him and hoped Paddy was more like him after he laughed out at this. As we walked back to the house, the smell of burning peat grew stronger, and we talked about Paddy and his ways. Uncle Mick, who was a very funny man who was always making me laugh and telling jokes, assured me that my relationship with him would improve as I grew older and that I wouldn't tell your Aunty Mary where you had been. He began to tell me about the tinkers, who only visit this cemetery once a year to pay respects to a young boy's grave. Then I understood that it must be the grave of the young man who was buried here all by himself the last time I came there.

The scent of the peat faded as we got closer to the farmhouse and was replaced by the aroma of Grandma's cooking. I hurried because I was so hungry, but Uncle Mick chuckled and said, "Slow down. Hopefully, we won't have to say grace."

After taking a seat at the table, we prayed briefly before beginning to eat. The meal included chicken, potatoes, mashed carrots, and swede. Before beginning to eat, I said an extra Hail Mary for the chicken because he had met his demise at the fate of the Red Wall. As I tasted the potatoes, which were different from those back home because they were so creamy and soft, I concluded that this is why the Irish eat potatoes with every meal. By accident, I skipped the carrots and swede. I was going to get up from the table when I was told to sit back down and stay until my plate was gone. When I was done, it was getting dark and time for bed.

When I told Uncle Mick in the morning where I was going to the tinkers, he said, "It's okay but don't go over the fence and don't be long," As I passed the donkey and moved toward the top field, I observed there was no smoke coming from where they were and patted the donkey. The only thing I could see when I peered down was an area of flattened grass, scattered with empty tins and other rubbish. It would be another year before they returned, and I would probably never see them again, which left me feeling quite unhappy. The donkey started to bray as he headed back down the field, and I passed him thinking he was laughing. I told him to be quiet and then I went to assist Uncle Mick with the cows who cheered me up with his comical ways.

The time was flying by, and I was spending the majority of it on the farm, harvesting hay, feeding chickens, and herding cows. Except for the time I spent with the Tinkers, it was quite a tedious job, so when it was time to say goodbye, I was happy to board the plane and look forward to returning to the English way of life. No wonder Paddy left home at such a young age, I thought. I was grateful that I still had five weeks of summer holiday when we returned to Oldham.

A.T.C.

Lena suggested we join the scouts or boys brigade, which at the time sounded a bit more mature than climbing the lows or playing football on the street, as there wasn't much to do during the holidays other than to be under her feet all day.

About four or five miles away further north was Saddleworth just past a little village called Lees on the edge of the then-Yorkshire border, to us it was a place where the rich people live in massive houses with huge gardens and new cars on the drives, people with their noses in the air looking down on you showing off their wealth as much as they could. It consisted of about four or five villages surrounded by the Yorkshire moors which were no man's land with beautiful scenery in the summer but a desolate dreary place in the winter.

one of the villages was called Uppermill on the local bus route and my mates and I used to visit it regularly usually in the summer holidays for something to do, on one of these visits we discovered the local ATC (air training corps) and decided to join, as a young lad of thirteen it was like joining the army with the opportunities and various things to do such as weekends away at an RAF camp, night exercises and a smart uniform appealed to us plus meeting new friends from all over the borough. I would take the number 4 bus to Uppermill Square and walk up the path to the ATC hut three evenings a week after finishing my studies. As I came closer, I could hear the band's bugles and drums playing a tune that made me think of troops marching to battle. After a few weeks, I got to know everyone and felt at home; it was a different atmosphere from the school where everyone was the same and we all worked as a team. At first, it was like starting a new job because, aside from a few of my friends, I didn't know anyone and the surroundings were a little strange.

Also, the various characters I encountered, such as the flight sergeant, who was a bit bossy but very comical with very big teeth and squinty eyes; we called him Tojo after the Japanese officer who served in the Second World War; corporal Cooper, who was the same as Jonesy in Dad's army and acted like him; and his friend, who reminded me of Private Walker from the same tv programme who always had something to sell and smoked a sly fag whenever he could. Tojo said I should play the drums since I tried to play the bugle but it made a scalded cat sound. When I showed up for band practice, I had anticipated learning the snare drum, but all of them had already been claimed. I was left playing the large bass drum, which was quite uncomfortable to wear at first but that I soon grew used to and loved. After a while, we had exercises to complete. One of these, named "Get Back," involved throwing us in the moors while blindfolded with enough food and drink to last us a day.

We set out early in the morning in a tractor and trailer that they borrowed from a nearby farmer, and after what seemed like an eternity, we arrived in the middle of nowhere. Tojo took charge and didn't take his eyes off the compass while stumbling along the damp meadow and arguing with Jonesy, who said we are going the wrong way. After some time, Tojo finally admitted we were lost. Jonesy wouldn't leave him alone, insisting that he was right and that all the boys were giving him stick, so he gave in and let Jonesy take charge. but by then the compasses were useless and the mist was coming down around us, we were all panicking for fear of being stuck on the moors all night until Tojo saw a little stream of water and we decided to follow which way the water was flowing to our surprise it started to get bigger and started to flow faster we continued for about two miles, the mist began to disappear and in the distance, we could hear a lot of rushing water and see the faint outline of Dovestones Reservoir situated on the outskirts of Greenfield a neighbouring village of Uppermill thank god we were safe but I didn't think Tojo was when Jonesy got him back to the hut and explained to the warrant officer.

Jonesey,s mate Sean who we nicknamed walker was always getting in trouble and was a bad influence on the group but he was a likeable lad and very popular with the lads. He was a bit of a Walter Mitty character and told us his dad owned a big store in Manchester, we did tend to believe him going off the various items he had on him to sell such as penknives and all sorts of gadgets mainly for self-survival and endurance plus he always had pocketfuls of fags,

We were all invited to the local scout troop in the nearby village of Diggle one day to compare the activities we all engaged in and perhaps pick one other's brains for some new ideas. It was a beautiful summer evening, so we went for a stroll with the scouts to the river that flowed through the village and relaxed at an embankment with a great pool of water that the locals called Diggle Dam. Walker was hesitant to go for some reason and seemed extremely nervous. We were all messing about on the side and Walker was whittling away with one of the penknives which I noticed had the scout emblem on it also the scout troop leader had his eyes on it and started to question him, we got back to base and he was hauled in the commander's office their hut had been broken into and Walker was one of the culprits, we never saw him again after that the last thing I heard he was in Strangeways and his dad's so-called cash and carry was a stall on Tommyfield market.

Following this episode, there was a large gathering in the hut with all the officers and non-commissioned officers to boost morale and separate the good guys from the bad. Three weeks before this, the annual 20-mile sponsored walk was held. Proceeds from the event went toward the purchase of our musical instruments, and the first four back-to-base received prizes. However, despite Jonesy's conduct with the officers, which gave the impression that he was a saint, the lads knew what he was about.

The walk went through various villages around Saddleworth with checkpoints every two miles where you would be handed a ticket to prove you had passed it, I was walking with my mate Mick and after about ten miles we noticed Jonesy well behind us down the lane as we passed the fourteen-mile checkpoint he was about a mile in front but he never passed us for a minute I thought he must have a twin brother and Mick who was more surprised than me noticed some writing on the back of one of the checkpoint tickets what said Michael Cooper and Co Printers. It turned out this was his uncle's company he had all the tickets in his pocket and he was taking shortcuts well that time it backfired on him he came fifth and won sod all he knew we found out but we didn't grass on him he calmed down a lot and he was a lot more friendly towards us after that.

Saddleworth was so different to what we were used to in Oldham it was like a different country with clean air and countryside there was no mill chimneys or cobbled streets with old ladies cleaning their doorsteps with donkey stones,there didn't seem to be any terraced houses just cottages surrounded by stone walls and wooden gates also everyone had a freshly cut lawn and flowers everywhere we often went round the back of the houses and always found the blackberry bushes were we picked the fruit hiding from the occupants who sometimes chased us back down the road to Lees,it was the best place to go blackberrying as we called it apart from the big old house on the side of the lows,the locals used to call it the manor house it was surrounded by wire fencing and guarded by two big fat bulldogs we usually found a hole in the fence and got in but the dogs sensed that we were there, as soon as our pockets were full they were onto us as well as the owner who came running when he heard the barking it was easy to get away the dogs were so slow they were that fat, plus the man who was chasing us who looked like he had eaten all of the pies in hollands bakery had no chance of catching us we had plenty of practise running away as a result of Paddy running after us when were in bother which was bound to happen when we got home with our faces and hands stained with blackberry juice and he knew what we had been up to.

As well as the teachers in the school Paddy was changing his way with me as I was growing up, the good hiding and the attitude towards me became a bit friendlier all the other kids my age had a bike and I was always pestering him to get me one which would make my paper round so much easier his answer was always that he couldn't afford it until one day he was sat in his chair when I came home from school he was in a very rare good mood calling me "moc" which is the Gaelic word for a son he only called me that when he was happy, Lena summoned me into the kitchen while he was laughing and making jokes with her, saying, "He's had a great win on the horses, ask him about the bike before he spends it at the pub or returns it to the bookie." To my surprise, he said, "Finish your round this evening and we'll go to the bicycle shop on Lees Road and put a deposit on one and pay it weekly out of your wages," even though I had lied when I asked him about it, saying that the paper round was so big in the morning that it was making me late for school. I would have to spend half of what I had made on the paper round, but getting a new bike seemed worthwhile. I understood that the lie I told my father was wrong, and I dreaded going to confession the following Saturday because I knew the priest would accuse me of breaking the fourth and seventh commandments—honouring my father and mother—as well as stealing the fruit from the wooden hut. I had anticipated having to say the Hail Mary as part of my penance for all eternity, but it was wonderful to ride my bike to church, so I didn't mind.

St Michael's

I was more terrified of Paddy's rage than I was of God's judgement. When I entered the confessional box on a Saturday and said the customary "Forgive me Father for I have sinned," the voice that answered me was very different from Father Hourigan's rough, almost shouting voice; it was gentle and much softer. I told Paddy when I got home, and he confirmed that St. Anne's had a new priest. We're going to St. Michael's starting now. I refrained from asking why out of concern for a backhander and the typical response of "don't ask questions." Lena later revealed to me that Paddy had been warned by someone that the new priest was becoming too friendly with the young boys. At the time, in my innocent mind, I didn't understand why there was anything wrong with the priest being friendly; instead, I was more concerned that Paddy would have to cross the dark side of the lows to get to St. Michael's and would have to find out what we were up to.

He would go to church in all kinds of weather; we would frequently see him battling the wind and rain through the upstairs window of Game Street. I used to think surely God wouldn't bother if you missed mass a few times. I frequently wondered what was going through his mind and what he was feeling. He had a habit of showing up at the wrong time, usually when we were about to light up a cigarette or some other devilment, as he called it. I was hesitant to ask him questions even though I had a lot of them. He must have had the typical attitude of a Catholic, which includes feelings of guilt, low self-esteem, and fear of the burning fires of hell, which you will burn for all eternity if a person does not turn from one's sins and live a modest life.

My loyalty to the Catholic Church and the values it upheld was put to the test. Even though it was being driven into me how magnificent and good this God was, I was unable to comprehend the agony and suffering that existed around the world and even in my neighbourhood. The secret tools used by Irish Catholics to get through life all fall under the category of "prayers."

The Hail Mary is the most important and widely used prayer; it is more of a guilt prayer. frequently accompanied by an act of penance to purge your soul of venial sin, such as telling white lies, swearing, and other minor misdeeds; depending on the severity, an odd Our Father may be added. For grave crimes like breaking one of the ten commandments, the Our Father (also known as the Lord's Prayer) and the Hail Holy Queen are frequently saved in the prayer bank. To express gratitude to God for everything they have in life, all of these prayers are uttered multiple times throughout the day. Additionally, they are used when saying the prayers before a meal, and the sign of the cross is frequently shown in public simply for show. The churches were packed on Sundays, and people knelt in the rear holding their prayer books and rosary beads while they absolved their consciences and begged for forgiveness for what had occurred the week before. returning home after mass with the knowledge that their sins had been forgiven and being able to enjoy their roast beef and Yorkshire pudding in peace.

For years the threat of the Devil and Hell was in my mind, not trying to do anything wrong or commit a sin for fear of this, but before that, there was the threat of Paddy and his belt. The least little thing I seemed to do against him was a sin. So to me when Paddy punished me on Earth I still had the wrath of God when I met him and if he judged me wrong the Devil was waiting. Growing up, my self-esteem was at an all-time low, and based on what I overheard from the others at school, the majority of them were as well. The children who were most afraid of the church's teachers, nuns, and priests were Irish or Anglo-Irish.

Holidays

Holiday outings in our household were very rare, it usually consisted of a day trip to Blackpool or if we were lucky we had a few days in a seaside apartment on the seafront at Rhyl in North Wales. Polly always came along with us to get some sea air and spend a bit of time with us but once the coach arrived and we got settled in we usually found her either at the bookies or playing the slot machines or the prize bingo in the arcades. If it were up to your dad, you would spend the day at Alexandra Park or an afternoon at the Glodwick Baths because at least he would save money on soap and water, Lena told me before we left. She had been holding back money from Paddy and saving it up so we could take a holiday. The majority of the time, we walked along the prom while smelling toffee apples and candy floss and hearing fairground sounds, aware that we would likely only be able to ride one ride each and share a stick of rock.

However, at least we were away from the street and Paddy's bad moods, which were at their worst during the school holidays. After about two days, the money Lena had attempted to budget had mostly disappeared. We would wait outside the bookies for Polly in the hopes that Lester Piggot had won so we could stay a little while longer. However, we were frequently disappointed; we could tell by her expression whether he had won or not. As a result, it was time to head back down to Yelloway bus station and board the old, non-air-conditioned coaches bound for Oldham.

Christmas and the holidays have always seemed to be difficult occasions, especially for my parents. The best thing to do was to stay out of Paddy's way and go out and come back when we were hungry. Paddy was home every day, and Lena frequently got on his nerves. We were constantly in and out of the house, making it impossible for him to study the form in the racing pages. He seemed happier when we were not there all the time, whereas Lena loved having us there and enjoyed our company.

My birthday which was in August coincided with the summer holidays and didn't seem that special, to me it was just another day thanks to Paddy's upbringing where I don't think they celebrated special occasions due to the number of children in his own family and how they struggled with money when they were younger, Lena, on the other hand, made sure we received a card and a bit of something. All the other kids had parties and loads of presents Lena would say "if your dad had a regular job and decent wages we would have the same" so we didn't complain and were thankful to save Lena from feeling sad for us.

Christmas holiday was a bit different in Paddy's eyes because he would repeatedly say "we are celebrating the birth of our Lord Jesus Christ" always followed by the sign of the cross which we had to say back to him and utter the collective "amen" usually in a hushed voice which would annoy him. He did make an effort to get us all a present though I don't know where they managed to find the money, especially in the winter when every other day he would be rained off or the roads were frozen up. On Christmas morning we would come downstairs to find our pile of gifts which consisted of one main present: a selection box, a comic book annual and an apple and orange. Paddy would be in bed nursing his hangover and Lena would be running around trying to keep us quiet in case he woke up, which he inevitably did as soon as we heard the creaking of the stairs we would disappear onto the street and watch enviously as the other kids were playing with their new toys or riding their bikes.

Around 10 o'clock Lena would call us in and tell us to get ready for mass amongst the usual complaining about why we had to go but one compensation was Paddy wasn't going he had been to midnight mass which was a yearly ritual for all the catholic drunks of the town to ease their conscience, where Father O'Leary, the new priest at St Michael's had cottoned on to this and halfway through the mass used to give them a right rollicking which didn't bother Paddy who knew the priest well and was certain it wasn't directed at him. Father

O, as Paddy referred to him, was another frequent visitor to the home and another occasion for us to move aside so they could talk about the pope or another matter of their faith. When Father O left, there was always an empty bottle of Irish whiskey on the table, and Paddy was in a good mood.

The positive attitudes were becoming less stable and spreading to the rest of us. Lena had changed, and I could tell that this would lead to more conflicts and friction within the family. We started to avoid Paddy more and more as my older brother started to rebel and go his own way.

Boxing

The neighbourhood boxing club was one of the things I would find to keep me away from the house. One of the school bullies was giving my friend Paul a lot of grief, so he encouraged him to settle it in the ring. I went to see it for myself and was astounded by the results. Even though the bully was twice Paul's size, he was knocked to the ground in the opening round and left with a bloodied nose. I joined the club that night and started to train three evenings a week. I told Paddy what I was doing but he was more interested in trying to pick the winners for the next day's racing in the evening chronicle and offered no encouragement. I carried on training at the club hoping for my first official fight which took a lot longer than I expected. I noticed the trainers were fathers of the lads who were getting the fights regular, when I mentioned this they said "We can't find a match with your age and weight.

But the favouritism persisted, so I came to terms with it. When my turn came, I accompanied them to a working men's club in Bradford. I lost my fight on points in front of roughly 200 drunken Yorkshire men who were cheering us on; it was an experience I'll never forget, but instead of making me feel upset, it motivated me even more to win my next fight. I improved my skills in the weeks that followed without assistance from the so-called trainers who were more interested in training their boys and learned how to box rather than engage in a street fight.

wherein the ring is restricted to fists. My preparation paid off, as I succeeded in my following five fights and began bringing trophies home, which Lena proudly exhibited on the sideboard. As the weeks went by with no sign of a competitive match, I began to feel as though my effort and hard work had been ignored and I realised I was not a member of the team. I was being used as cannon fodder while sparring with the more seasoned older fighters, despite the trainers' assurances that it was all part of your training. I decided that the gym already had enough punch bags and called it quits.

The school was getting a lot easier mainly because it was the last year I had to be there, plus the older kids had left and the teachers had more time for us. It was 1972 Bowie, T Rex and Elton John were never off the radio and all sorts of so-called American artists such as The Osmonds and David Cassidy started to hit the charts. Most of my mates left at Easter that year, I wasn't fifteen until August so I was about to leave in the summer and it couldn't come soon enough. All through my last year at school, apart from looking forward to leaving, was about doing the things I wanted to do instead of what Paddy, the church and the teachers wanted.

Leaving School

On July 22, 1972, Lean on me, a song by Bill Withers, peaked at number one. I was released into the big wide world of work on this day, and Ted Heath was still the prime minister leading a right-wing government. Right-wing in a political context confused me because the only right-wing I was familiar with was on a bird or Georgie Best. I had to go ask the one teacher in the school I trusted for an explanation. The manner he taught me was similar to a see-saw, with left on one side and right on the other, aiming to achieve the ideal balance in the middle, which never happened in government or in real life. His subject was English, although he was skilled in many disciplines. I would have remained there all day but luckily the bell rang before he began to bore me about Karl Marx. With the rich and better-off people in life on the right and the weak and vulnerable people on the left, I came to the conclusion that each side wanted to remove the other from their current situation. This was visible in the classroom, where the teachers seemed to give the best instruction and attention to the pupils who were better-groomed and whose parents held respectable professions. My determination to leave this school as soon as possible was increased by this. It was such a relief to leave school on the last day, especially since the teachers' favourite students had brought them gifts and sweets and cake. They were preparing for an afternoon party. I didn't want to show my face, but I needed to get my final report, so I sneaked out early, passing a couple of students who were crying, and I felt like jumping for joy. I imagined the shock they would feel if they went into the working environment of Oldham without the protection of the teachers who had given them the most attention and been gentle with every mistake or weakness they displayed. I went back to Game street and sat in the back room and gazed at the flames in front of the old coal fire with the eyes of Jesus following my every move and watched as it burned my report into ashes. I thanked him that I didn't have to go to that awful place again but also questioned him about why he put me there in the first place.

Work and the pub

I was ready to start work, but I had to wait until my fifteenth birthday, which was on August 2. It was a temporary labour position till I began my apprenticeship in September and it was located at a handbag factory where my sister also worked. It consisted of taking the work to rows of sewing machinists who were all women and being a young lad was teased endlessly as I delivered the materials to them. I took it in my stride knowing my embarrassment would only last a few weeks and looked forward to my next employers in the trailer manufacturers.

The company's name was Crane Fruehauf. About 2000 workers were employed there in Oldham by the German firm. When I got to the factory, they told me I had to spend my first year in an engineering training school on the opposite side of town in Bardsley. As soon as they mentioned school, I immediately thought, "Not another year of dull teachers," but then I reminded myself that this was supposed to be my job and that I would be paid this time, so it can't be all that horrible. When I arrived on the first day, that assumption was proven false.

I walked down the cobbled street towards the entrance where there was a queue of young lads waiting to clock in. It reminded me of my old school with the pupils lining up to go to the assembly, but they weren't any teachers and to my surprise, they called me by my first name. At last, someone is treating me like an adult I thought as I tried my overalls on and put a cap on supposedly keeping my hair hidden in case it got wrapped around the machinery.

I felt like a walking shamrock in the dark green overalls, and I knew Paddy would approve. The first day was all about health and safety; I learned what I already knew in the classroom, which was just common sense. After a few weeks, I felt at home and made some friends named Dennis and Phil. As usual, one of them was a good guy, while the other was a menace who had a name that rhymes with menace. Dennis, who was a little older than us and had a strong personality, would frequently bring Phil and me into the nearby pub during our lunch break.

The pub was called the Black Diamond and the landlord would turn a blind eye when Dennis ordered three pints of brew ten bitter and three Hollands pies. On the way home to save on bus fare, all three of us would walk home. Opposite the works was a street that led to an area called park bridge which consisted of a lot of farms and countryside, if we walked as the crow flies we would end up in Alt estate which was where Dennis and Phil lived and of course, Dennis knew a shortcut which involved us running over various farmers fields being chased by the farmer and his dogs.

Luckily we were faster and the thought of saving the bus fare was worth it. After I Left them I would often call at Mick's greengrocer's shop where he would be helping his mother with the tea time rush. When he had finished we would call at his house for a brew. He often put an album on his dad's old record player whilst we drank about three or four of his mother's brews,s and demolished the tin of biscuits. It was the same LP he would play over and over.

The musician was Bob Dylan, an American who had a significant impact on the youth of the USA and appeared to start having an impact on us.

Although I don't think Dylan was a particularly excellent singer or musician, I was interested in what he was singing about. He was an excellent poet and songwriter, and he frequently wrote about the women, girls, and friends in his life in addition to the challenges and sorrows of the world and the people who live in it.

One day I called at Mick's and as I knocked on his door I could hear the usual gritty whining voice of Dylan on the record player and Mick was singing along with him trying to strum his new guitar which he had bought the previous day. The attempts at trying to master the two chords of E and A minor stopped and he let me in, put the kettle on and showed off his new instrument, also how he was progressing, he had managed to play the chords and apart from the occasional buzzing sound where his fingers caught the strings but I was impressed how quickly he had learned to change them.

This inspired me and I thought if he can do this in that amount of time well so can I. My wages wouldn't stretch to buying a new one so I had a word with a schoolmate of mine whose father owned a second-hand shop in the town centre called Aladdin's cave. You could buy anything in this shop. golf clubs, old prams, and musical instruments. It was a place where the people would sell items when they were a bit desperate for a bit of cash, The neighbourhood drunks would frequently line up to sell their wares so they could buy a few more pints at the pub. There were about three or four guitars in the store. Fortunately, there was an acoustic with a missing string, which they let me have for twenty pounds. I then had to go up to the music store to buy a set of strings while wandering about pretending to be a rockstar.

As I walked down the street I had my guitar in hand and was thinking all sorts with my imagination running away with me about how I could form a band. When I realised that I had no idea how to play it, let alone how to attach the strings or tune it. I assumed it would take years for someone to learn how to play an instrument, and my assumption was confirmed when I got to Mick's place and tried to put the new strings on, Mick taught me how to tune it and put the strings on, which was a lot tougher than I anticipated. I had mistakenly believed that this was more difficult than learning a few chords.

After approximately an hour of fitting the new strings, I was able to tune the instrument and try out a few notes. I could only hear buzzing where my fingers contacted the other strings.

We agreed to practise for at least an hour every evening after work. Learning to change two chords at once took me a long time. However, the buzzing soon subsided, and I was able to capture what appeared to be a musical note. When I could, I would practise in the living room while I waited for my older brother to finish his Frank Zappa L.P. or my sister to start playing her Motown album.

The first time I took my guitar home and started practising Paddy wasn't too happy with the noise coming from the front room. especially considering that the next week I purchased my first Bob Dylan L.P. He informed Lena that I sounded like a scalded cat and that the man on the record player's singing was far worse.

He'd be gone to the pub the moment he spotted me entering the living room and picking it up. I was encouraged by Lena to practise simply to get him out of the house.

Because my older brother, sister, and I were now responsible for paying for our board, bringing money to the house improved my relationship with my father a little. Paddy was able to spend more time in the pub and appeared to be much happier as a result. There were still a lot of tense moments, but they weren't as bad as they had been, and I was beginning to relax in his company.

It was Christmas of 1973. Ted Heath was still prime minister, and things were getting worse. He was about to institute a three-day week, and the miners threatened to strike, which they did in late January 1974, leaving the country in chaos. Work at the trailer factory was becoming increasingly limited. I couldn't believe how powerful the unions were; any kind of dispute and we were on strike, filling Shaw rd like fans leaving Old Trafford. We would only return once we had got what we wanted.

As a result, the trailer park was becoming full, with no orders coming in and employees were spreading rumours of cutbacks and shorter hours. Overtime was prohibited, and no new employees were hired. My job seemed to be in jeopardy here, and the inevitable redundancies began. I was one of the first people on the list to go, as it was done on a last-in-first-out basis. But they didn't take in the fact I was an apprentice which at the time was against employment law rules. The convener summoned me to the union office to tell me about a meeting with my manager. We went into the meeting, and he threatened to go on strike unless I was immediately reinstated.

They caved in almost immediately, and my job was saved. I realised then how much power the people and unions had in the early 1970s when they were willing to bring the entire place to a standstill for the sake of a sixteen-year-old's job. Working in the factory opened my eyes to a lot of things, especially listening to the older workers and their life experiences, as well as their sense of humour, which was always on the adult side. As the saying goes, the three major topics were wine, women, and song. Because they were northern working class, the first one, 'wine,' would be changed to beer, either bitter or mild, or a combination of the two. No one drank Lager because it was for the women who would turn into birds or a bit of crumpet. As for the song, it would be anything catchy they heard on the radio, which would be played on overhead speakers throughout the works if you could hear it over the noise.

Throughout this time, Prime Minister Ted Heath resigned, paving the way for a Labour Government, and Harold Wilson took over, much to the delight of the unions, and sorted out the miners. This did not save my job, as I was laid off and the factory eventually closed. Fortunately, I found work quickly and began working at the garage in Hollinwood, servicing the waggons and vans for Park Cake bakeries. I believe my Aunty Doris 'the one we called chicken leg Doris' was a supervisor, and had put in a good word for me. About 20 lads worked here, and they all enjoyed a pie and a pint at dinnertime in the local pub, where I first tasted a decent pint of bitter.   I was sixteen and a half years old when I discovered pubs where landlords turned a blind eye to underage drinkers; they were usually the ones whose takings were low and needed the business. My favourite watering hole was the Highfield and Park on Waterloo Street; it was cheap, the beer was decent, and it was a long way from Paddy's local. He was a creature of habit, always loyal to the landlord of the nearest pub. I was new to the effects of alcohol, and it was a real challenge and a lot of acting when I got home to hide the fact that I was under the influence of it. I think he knew I was but ignored it to avoid starting a fight, Lena always said 'if you work hard all day you are entitled to a bit of time in the pub' at the time I think she was referring to when I was legally old enough to buy a pint, but that would have been my argument if Paddy had said anything that would have resulted in the two of them arguing.

Oldham brewed its beer, known locally as OB, which was the best-tasting beer in the northwest. It was all real ale brewed in cask barrels and hand-drawn from the pumps in their popular local pubs. They were always in competition with one of Manchester's breweries Wilson's, whilst Wilson's had a range of bottled ales and keg beers OB were exclusive to their own. I preferred OB bitter which was the nectar of the gods, the lager on the other hand was called Rheingold where you had to have either lime or blackcurrant juice to kill its bitter and sour taste.

Paddy didn't seem to care about me much now that I was working, but his legacy of the Catholic church weighed heavily on my shoulders, as did the guilt I felt if I did anything wrong. Even swearing or arguing with Lena would be met with a couple of Hail Marys to ease my conscience. Mass on Sunday was still one of his rules while I was living with him, but it was easily resolved by taking an hour-long walk around the lows. Lena, on the other hand, wasn't particularly religious and occasionally joined me. I couldn't understand why I had to stand, kneel, and pray every Sunday morning with a large group of people, most of whom I didn't even know, with a priest telling me how I should live my life. It also reminded me of my mistakes while filling me with fear of the consequences if I didn't.

When people began walking down the side of the lows in their best clothes, I knew it was time to go home. With the sound of bells peeling out from St Marks, a protestant church seemed to finish its service at the same time. It always seemed strange how well-dressed people were at church; if you weren't, you were frowned upon. Nonetheless, they preached about how God cared about all of us, rich or poor, but make sure you are very smart when you come to my church.

I was 17 years old and motivated to pass my driving test because I thought that getting a driver's licence would open up a lot of work opportunities for me. such as running a taxi or doing deliveries. My older brother gave me the name of an instructor he had lessons with because he was very affordable and skilled at what he did. The first time behind the wheel was a little unsettling, but because he had dual control, he was actually in charge. After a few classes, I gained confidence and began to drive without being instructed. Because of his busy schedule, the instructor would occasionally nod off while I was driving. When I would frantically try to wake him up, he would reply, "I was awake the entire time I was testing you to see whether you could handle the car on your own.' This was a bit of a wake-up call, and I assumed that this was why he was so cheap, so I stopped taking lessons from him and switched to a recognised driving school. Although they cost twice as much, I decided that my life was worth the few extra pounds I ultimately passed on my third attempt, which seemed like a tremendous relief and triumph to me after countless lessons and two failed tests. There were many options available while looking for a job that required a driving licence. This would be useful given the rising unemployment rates in the UK

At seventeen years old, somewhere between adulthood and childhood, things in my body and mind were changing and becoming very confusing, which I seemed to accept. All of my so-called school friends had mostly vanished, but I felt like a free agent doing the things I liked, while Paddy's Power remained in the background. It reminded me of the Catholic Church and what it stood for: feeling guilty, unworthy of making a name for yourself, being wealthy, or being famous. It was drilled into me that if you work hard, find a girl, marry, have children, and don't sin, God will reward you in Heaven when your life is over. However, if you commit a sin, you will be punished on earth as well as burned in hell when you die.

I was battling an inner voice in my head that told me what was right and wrong in certain situations. I confided in Lena about this, and her response was, 'you are becoming a man, and making decisions is part of that.' This, I believe, is her way of saying that you must now deal with these issues in your way, without your Catholic conscience interfering. There was no point in asking Paddy because every piece of advice I asked him, every problem I had, and every good idea I had was always the opposite of what I said and was dealt with negatively.

On my days off and weekends, I would frequently take the local train and travel to the villages and areas that surrounded Oldham, stopping at local pubs and cafes. It was good to see new places and meet new people. I was fortunate to appear a few years older than I was, so going to pubs and clubs was no problem, and some of the places I visited had an interesting local history and rivalry with their neighbouring village. I learned that the locals in these areas didn't react well to outsiders, so I had to be quite careful about who I talked to. It seemed as though I was trespassing on their turf because they were so proud of where they came from

The Army

Due to the recession in the UK, the new place I was working was not doing so well after the first few months I was there but it survived until around my eighteenth birthday where once again I was made redundant and I began to think about the future and the possibility of being out of work. Jobs were becoming scarce, and I was considering joining the military. So it was back on the local train to the rainy city, where I entered the army careers office on Deansgate Manchester. Where I was greeted by a terrifying uniformed man with a deep, craggy voice who questioned me about my school and the companies I had worked for. He gave me an appointment for a medical the next day, filled out a few forms, and said to me before I left, 'Don't worry son, we take anyone on here, the army will make you a man.' The rapidity of it all made me wonder if they were desperate for lads to join.

This reminded me of Tom Leech being recruited to join the First World War all those years ago, but it didn't deter me, and the next day I took and passed the medical, where I was given a date to report and sign the papers the following week. Paddy was taken aback by the news, and he assumed and was probably correct, that I would be sent to Northern Ireland. The troubles were getting worse, and he was genuinely concerned for my safety, which I assumed was why the officer was trying to recruit me so quickly.

Paddy returned home from work the following Friday, just a few days before I was to be enlisted, and said he had spoken with the foreman at his works and they needed a labourer. If I wanted the job, I could start on Monday, so I said yes. To be honest, I wasn't particularly interested in the army; it was just the prospect of being unemployed that caught my attention. Later, Lena told me that he was so concerned about me joining the army that he practically begged the foreman to take me on.

I thought it would be interesting to work with my father and learn more about Paddy's personality, but I could tell from the first day that he was always on high alert. Rather than acting like a father and son, he was acting more like an employee. I thought Paddy was behaving maturely because he was acting as if the roles had been reversed and I was the adult there. Paddy was very quiet. In my presence, he was not participating at all as the other staff were joking about, swearing, and discussing the wife and what had occurred in the pub over the weekend. At that point, I realised he isn't as strong as I had believed, just a normal guy trying to provide for his family and raise his kids the way he was raised. Maybe I thought this was the beginning of the end of Paddy's Power.

Because the factory I worked at was at the far end of town, Paddy and I had to be picked up in the morning by his friend Harold, who lived just around the corner on Roundthorn Road. He was almost ready to retire and drove an old grey Morris Minor van to transport his homing pigeons. Paddy handed me an old newspaper and said, "Spread this in the back of the van when you get in so you don't sit on the bird shit" on the first day as we waited outside his house for him to get ready in the freezing cold. This was the first time I'd heard him say anything resembling a swear word. I realised then that I was being thrown in the back like one of Harold's smelly old pigeons. We drove to the factory, with Harold talking about his time in the army and Paddy trying to get a word in after each puff of his first Woodbine of the day, which was wafting in the back and making me cough, especially when it mixed with the smell of the pigeons. We arrived at the factory safely after about two woodbines and plenty of signs of the cross from Paddy. When I met the foreman and my work partner Bill, a big, chubby, balding man in his fifties who seemed to know everything about everything, Paddy said, "Take anything Bill says with a pinch of salt." "He's a bit of a romancer, but he's alright." Paddy was correct. When I first met Bill, it was difficult to find anything he hadn't seen or done, but once I got to know him, he was fine. I assumed he was acting this way because he was lonely and trying too hard to impress people, which didn't always work. My job was his labourer while he was spraying paint on all the components they made at the works, which I thought was temporary so I could put up with it. Lena was not pleased when I arrived home on the first day smelling of paint and thinners; I feared it would kill a few of Harold's pigeons as we drove home in his van with the windows open. I made it through the rest of the week and began to enjoy the job and Bill's company. Every now and then, Paddy would drop by to see how I was doing; he frequently slipped up and swore, which caused a bit of embarrassment between us as his face turned red.

I felt as though a huge weight had been lifted off of my shoulders the moment I clocked out on the Friday night of the first week of working at the same factory as Paddy. I felt like an adult once I proved to him how hard I worked and how well I got along with the other workers. At that point, he started treating me like one of them. I thought I might be able to enjoy the freedom of my remaining youth after his attitude abruptly changed.

Rugby

It was 1975. Harold Wilson was still in office as prime minister, and the troubles in Northern Ireland were keeping him busy. Also, the hooligans on the terraces were posing serious problems for both the police and the devoted fans. The football season was already well underway. Although I wasn't a huge fan of football, my younger brother and I had always enjoyed rugby, so I decided to join the local Rugby League team. The team's name was Waterhead. They trained on Tuesday and Thursday and played on Saturday afternoons. My younger brother made the choice to play in Saddleworth for a competing team. I wasn't good enough at the time to make the first team because I didn't have a lot of experience, but I was frequently selected for the A team. I recognized a few of the lads I played with because they were all locals who attended the same schools as me. I wouldn't mess with many of them because they looked like tough, useful lads. But I quickly realised that they were on my side, and the comradery was fantastic, especially during a game.

The club was a massive green shed, and aside from the bright paint, which I assumed was a loan from the town council because I knew some of the guys worked there, it reminded me of the old barn in Irishtown. I discovered at the time that the team, which included painters, joiners, and probably every other type of tradesperson you could imagine, was responsible for building it. The bar, which resembled the neighbourhood pub, was the first thing I observed as I entered the building. To the side of the bar, there was a door leading to the changing areas, which had an aura of wintergreen and what I assumed to be menthol. Two shared bathrooms, one for the home team and one for the visiting team, were located at the back of the room. They resembled two large concrete squares with a shower on one side. I had the instant thought that I would have to share this bathroom with at least 14 other men. My initial reluctance was immediately gone after the first training session, when the entire team decided they didn't care and swiftly got in the shower to wash off the sweat and grime they had accumulated. I realised why they were so quick when I eventually made it to the bar, the queue was a mile long, but it was worth it when I got to the bar and happily downed a pint of Tetley's bitter.

When Saturday finally arrived, I was chosen for the squad, but I don't believe it was because of my exceptional skill in the game since there weren't quite enough players. My faith in the Catholic Church was still present, and I found myself doing the sign of the cross and quickly mumbling a few Hail Marys under my breath before the game started. We played a team from Halifax named Siddall Rangers; I was in the second row. We got a real beating because they were one of the toughest teams in the league. Whether it was the first or second tackle, I had the responsibility—if you could call it that—of driving the ball in to weaken their forwards. My first try at this resulted in a bloody nose; it felt like I had run into a brick wall, but it seemed to work as when we lost the ball, they were unable to quickly cover the backs. This didn't last very long since they continued scoring and we weren't as fit as we thought we were. My body felt as though I had just fought ten rounds with a heavyweight boxer as we all made our way back to the changing rooms after the game, sad but not defeated, and saying a few Hail Marys to thank God for not being seriously injured. As we sat in the locker rooms and received a rollicking from the coach, we were feeling anything but dejected. I had pain all over, and when my teammate Pete noticed that I was a little uncomfortable, he reassured me that a few pints of Tetley's pain reliever would take care of the problem. After the game, the customary bath was taken, and my team competed with its rivals by singing louder than them. Pete remarked, "Always remember the team's motto," as I began to towel off and change. " Win or lose, have a booze" which made me feel a bit better, and we proceeded to the bar. The Tetleys started kicking in after a few pints, and I felt a lot better as we talked about how we played and how to improve in between a few games of cards and darts. Then it was back home to get washed and scrubbed before hitting the town. I was surprised to hear Paddy ask how we got along when I got home, bruised and battered. Mind you, he had just finished his lunchtime session in the pub, which I know a couple of the lads' fathers frequent, but he did seem genuinely interested, especially when he asked about my younger brother's team.

I always ate something before the players met at the Hare and Hounds pub in town because Paddy always said never to drink on an empty stomach, which was sound advice I couldn't argue with, but the arguments at Game Street were getting worse. We were all growing up, and privacy was a big problem. It was starting to get a bit overcrowded, and I often thought it was time to find a place of my own. This thought soon left my mind when I knew there was no way I could afford it with the wages I was earning at Paddy's Works.

Freedom

After a few months of working with Paddy and not being able to be myself or behave in the way I wanted, I decided to look elsewhere. I was grateful for the opportunity to earn some money, but the working conditions were appalling. Breathing in the paint fumes every day was giving me chest pains, Bill was getting on my nerves, and I was sure Paddy was watching me to make sure I wasn't letting him down. There were few jobs available, orders at the plant were slowing down, and there was less work to be done overall. Rumours of redundancies were circulating, and I knew my name would be first on the list. When the foreman gave me my redundancy notice right before I left work on Friday, I knew my suspicions were well-founded. Paddy was alright because he had been there for a while; therefore, he managed to live and continue, but for me, it was back to the job centre. I was back competing with the unemployed for the few job vacancies the following week. On August 2, 1975, I turned eighteen and made friends with a landlord's son I met in Werneth on the other side of town, who told me his father needed a part-time barman. I realised the extra money would help pay for my rent when I finally moved out, as well as save me money drinking in the pub. I got the job and started working the next Monday evening at six o'clock. The landlord was an Oldham Brewery tenant who took excellent care of his beer, and the pub was well-known in the area for serving one of the best pints of ale in town. Clara, one of his barmaids in her fifties, showed me the ropes and how to pull a pint. Clara handled the beer with care, as if she were teasing it through the pumps from the barrel to the glass. My first attempt was a disaster, with beer all over the place, but I persevered and eventually managed to pull a pint. Clara had been doing this for years and had perfected it; as a result, she was a favourite with the customers, who preferred to wait for her rather than be served by someone else. I paid close attention to how she pumped the beer and listened to her as she mentally calculated the cost of the drinks. She was muttering while she did this, and I frequently assumed that she was speaking to me, but she later clarified that she was adding up the amount as she went along. Over time, customers began to trust me to serve them a good pint and my tips began to add up, all of which helped me reach my goal of earning enough money to leave Game Street. At the pub, I met a lot of interesting people; it was the kind of place where workers would stop for a few pints before heading home.I couldn't believe how much they could drink, or that they were drinking it as quickly as I was pulling pints.

My older sister worked in Bradbury's woollen mill office in Uppermill, Saddleworth, and spoke with the manager about hiring me. Many employers in the 1970s would hire you based on who you knew rather than what you knew. Almost every factory or business had two or three members of a family working there. She came home one day and told me to see the manager on Monday about a job in the maintenance department. I was a bit concerned about this because of my previous experience working at the factory with Paddy. I reminded myself that I would need to be on my best behaviour for the sake of my family. The following morning, I got ready and put on my one and only suit. I then caught a bus for a half-hour ride to Uppermill, where I entered the office feeling a little nervous. Everything was so informal that I didn't need to be concerned, and my worries weren't justified. The manager was a cousin of the owner, named Hamilton Bradbury. When I first met him, he shook my hand and said, "Welcome to the firm, we are very relaxed here, there are no formalities, and everybody calls me Hammy" before giving me a tour of the mill. I couldn't believe I hadn't even answered a question yet and I got the job based on my sister's reputation and recommendation. The mill looked a lot brighter and cleaner than the old red brick mills that were scattered across Oldham. Various casement windows that were probably shut most of the time to block out noise were featured in the stone-built bricks.

As soon as I entered, Hammy detailed every step and its related outcome. Bales of wool that had been dyed beforehand in all sorts of colours were first delivered to a large area known as the card room. The wool was flattened, twisted, and compressed inside by giant rollers in order to prepare it for spinning. It was so loud that Hammy was doing his best to explain what was happening, but I was unable to understand him. Nevertheless, I had an idea, so we went upstairs to the spinning room, which was much quieter. The wool was brought into the room on big "bobbins," as they called them, and was spun onto smaller 'bobbins,' which were then brought up to the next floor and wound onto cones in preparation for the weaving shed. After the weavers finished their work, they produced countless rolls of tartan cloth featuring various Scottish clans, which were then delivered there and sold to the Scots. This surprised me a little and made me think that it would be like selling ice to the Eskimos or sand to the Arabs.

Everyone I worked with was friendly, and they all claimed to be from Yorkshire and were rather proud of it, despite the Lancashire border being just about two miles away. I felt comfortable here. I was liberated from Paddy's continuous scrutiny and allowed to be myself. My responsibility was to assist Jerry in the maintenance department with repairs and building upkeep in general. Jerry was a middle-aged man with a thick Yorkshire accent. It amused me how quickly the dialect changed compared to where I was living. The fact that there weren't many young men or women working here stuck out as I walked about the mill and spoke to various employees. Oldham's cotton mills were failing, so perhaps the younger generation didn't see a future for them. I met a number of odd and interesting characters who appeared to make the job easier as I got to know people in the mill. Lena recalled how it brought back memories of her time working in the mills following the war when I told her about it.When I informed her about it, she would get a bit tearful and Paddy would comfort her by telling her that it was all over. It was one of the few times I had ever seen them show affection for one another.

Paddy was surprised every morning when I would be up early, but I looked forward to going, so the early mornings didn't bother me. Before we started working, Harry and I would enjoy each other's company, have a good laugh, and crack the occasional joke as soon as I arrived. He shared a rented house in Uppermill with another friend, and they had a spare room. He offered me the room after hearing about my home situation and said, "It would be a lot cheaper to live if we split it three ways." I went home and told Lena what he had said, and she said, "I'll be sorry to see you go, but you are old enough to make your own decisions." She added, " I don't think your father would be bothered, so it's up to you " It didn't take me long to think about it, so I took him up on his offer and moved in at the weekend. Even though I had my parents blessing I still had feelings of guilt and letting them down, Paddy's Power seemed to have disappeared but the influence of the church was still there.

AMEN

Printed in Great Britain
by Amazon